SINGLE DIGIT YOUTH GROUPS

Working With Fewer Than 10 Teens

Marcey Balcomb

SINGLE DIGIT YOUTH GROUPS

Working With Fewer Than 10 Teens

Marcey Balcomb

04 05 06 07 08 09 10 11 12 13—10 9 8 7 6 5 4 3 2 1

Cover design: Keely Moore.

Dedicated
to the youth, families, and churches of
Common Cup Youth Ministry, Portland, Oregon.
It is a real joy being in ministry together.
Thank you for your faithful support and
all of the great experiences we've had.

You're the best!

Contents

Fewer Than Ten

In today's society, youth can choose from myriad of activities in which to participate. They have great learning opportunities such as sports, music, language and science programs, and scouting. Since many schools and teams no longer set aside Wednesday night or Sunday as family and church time, youth are often asked to choose between participation in those areas or church. Sometimes their grades or credits at school require their attendance at times that conflict with church activities.

So how do we keep youth interested in and committed to being part of a church community? What do we offer that can possibly outweigh the appeal of the other opportunities? Why would they want to choose church instead? Who is responsible for providing ways to help youth feel they are wanted and they belong in the church?

Do you have fewer that ten active youth in your congregation? If you do, you still have potential for a youth ministry program to support those youth. And if you already have a youth single-digit youth group, I hope this book will refresh your commitment to keeping that opportunity alive for them so that they can grow in the faith.

Youth who are open to the exploration of faith usually want to experience God in their lives, not just hear or talk about God. While it is possible for them to live out this journey in isolation, it more likely occurs if they have spent previous time in study, conversation, searching, and wondering. Adolescence is the key time for the church community to play a primary role in guiding young people in developing intentional lifestyles of faith. We can provide experiences that keep their interest while walking beside them on their journey.

The American Heritage Dictionary defines the word *experience* as "active participation in events or activities, leading to the accumulation of knowledge or skill." Experiential learning, then, means learning by observing, hearing, seeing, or doing something. We can help youth explore their faith by providing opportunities for them to not only discuss and think about God but also to experience God.

> It isn't the numbers that matter. It's each and every teenager we are entrusted with to help them grow into disciples of the living Christ.

Every young person is important. If we provide youth groups and other programs for large numbers of youth, why would we not provide programs for smaller numbers of youth? I firmly believe that if you have even one, two, or three youth who can meet together in some way then you can have a youth group. After all, good things often come in small packages or, in this case, small numbers! Despite what we are sometimes told, it isn't the numbers that matter. It's each and every teenager we are entrusted with to help them grow into disciples of the living Christ.

This book includes benefits, strategies, and practical helps in beginning or strengthening single-digit youth groups, as well as Scripture-based activities and short stories of what has worked for me and for others. A variety of reproducible forms are also provided for your use or adaptation. I hope you will find this book useful in discovering what it means to be in ministry with youth, even when there are only a few.

And if you have a head start by already having a single-digit youth group, great! Maybe this book will give you a boost and some new ways to guide youth in exploring their faith.

Each and every youth in our churches needs and deserves our support and encouragement as they grow and change. This book offers some ways to be there for them on that journey, regardless of the size of the group.

There are many successes to be accomplished through this effort. Come, join the journey!

1

Single-Digit Youth Groups: Founded in Scripture

Two or Three, Plus One

> For where two or three are gathered in my name, I am there among them. (Matthew 18:20)

God's presence is something we can count on regardless of how many people are meeting. We often open a gathering with prayer, inviting God to be with us during our time together. While I am sure that God appreciates hearing our invocation, God is there whether specifically invited or not. It's up to us to acknowledge God's presence and to be open to the guidance of the Spirit as we go about our session. God is so much more than we can even begin to imagine.

Sometimes I am even more amazed that God uses individuals, such as me, to carry on the work among God's people and among all we have been given to enjoy and watch over. What a privilege! This call is also a huge responsibility, and I don't always feel up to the challenge. Yet here we are, people of God, called to share the good news and help others find their way to a relationship or a deeper relationship with God.

The church must therefore guide others in becoming disciples of Jesus Christ. How can we possibly take on such an awesome responsibility when we may not feel adequate, let alone skilled, for the task? The answer is actually quite simple: We walk beside others on their journey, one by one. Every youth we have access to deserves the opportunity to learn, grow, and be cared for with the love of God.

A certain level of excitement and power is no doubt a part of having a larger, "critical mass" of people. We certainly need to find ways for our youth to celebrate their faith with other groups of Christian youth. But week to week we should care for the few who are there. If you have a single-digit youth group or any youth in your congregation or neighborhood, the same privilege and responsibility are yours.

So while increasing numbers of participants is nice and often expected by others in the congregation, we shouldn't waste the chance to work with those we already have. Jesus' example and message calls us to be fishers of all people, bringing them close to the heart of God. If you have even one or two youth and an adult willing to gather in the name of Jesus Christ, then he is among you.

Sometimes, Just One

In youth ministry we have a unique opportunity to use experiential teaching to help youth experience God among us. Not every youth we work with will grasp or hold onto what we try to teach; but if they are open and willing to learn, we can at least plant and water the seeds so that they can grow at their own pace. We often plant seeds that may take years to sprout, but we need to trust that they will grow whether we will see them or not. If we wait for proof that our ministry is effective with every youth, we will be quickly discouraged.

> Every youth deserves the opportunity to learn, grow, and be cared for with the love of God.

Michelle, who graduated from our group, came by to visit the youth group. While reminiscing about her years in the youth group, she asked if I remembered "our day" at the zoo. This day was the second month of our brand-new youth program, and we had scheduled a day together at the zoo for group building. I was there early so that I could greet the youth as they arrived. Michelle got there and waited with me for the others, but no one else came. So I told her I was prepared to spend this time with her but that she had the option of staying or going home guilt free. She wanted to stay, and we had a great day together.

As she told this story to some of our younger youth, she paused at the end and said: "Your youth director spent the entire day with me—just me—and I'll never forget how important that made me feel. She could have legitimately cancelled the event, but she didn't. I think I talked the whole day, and she actually listened to me. After that, I tried to be at every meeting so I could give back the support she gave me."

As it turned out, that day could not have been more critical for a large group than it was for the one youth who came. It set a foundation for Michelle's five more years in our program, helping her build the trust she needed to open up and explore her faith within a new youth group.

Only Twelve

Jesus called only twelve disciples to follow him, accompany him in his travels, and learn from him. He didn't look for the most popular, intelligent, or interested people for the job. He called ordinary people from diverse communities and professions, just as God continues to call people today. Matthew 4:18-22 describes how Jesus called the first disciples:

> As he walked by the Sea of Galilee, he saw two brothers, Simon, who is called Peter, and Andrew his brother, casting a net into the sea—for they were fishermen. And he said to them, "Follow me, and I will make you fish for people." Immediately they left their nets and followed him. As he went from there, he saw two other brothers, James son of Zebedee and his brother John, in the boat with their father Zebedee, mending their nets, and he called them. Immediately they left the boat and their father, and followed him.

From there Jesus traveled and taught those he met along the way by telling stories or parables. He healed the sick and performed other miracles, drawing the attention of huge crowds of people who came to see him. Many brought friends and relatives in hopes that Jesus would heal them also. Jesus continued to call disciples even as he returned to his home town:

> As Jesus was walking along, he saw a man called Matthew sitting at the tax booth; and he said to him, "Follow me." And he got up and followed him. (Matthew 9:9)

> Then Jesus went about all the cities and villages teaching in their synagogues, and proclaiming the good news of the kingdom, and curing every disease and every sickness. (Matthew 9:35)

With a single-digit youth group, you can call each person by name. For some youth, just knowing that they are noticed and that they matter can be the greatest gift.

With fewer than ten teens, you can go fishing and discuss how Jesus gathered only twelve disciples to accompany him and learn the work he would ask them to continue in his name. This task often confused and frustrated the disciples, who constantly asked Jesus what his parables meant. He liked to answer questions with questions, and they searched deeper for understanding.

> With a single-digit youth group, you can call each person by name. For some youth, just knowing that they are noticed and that they matter can be the greatest gift.

Being able to take a small group of youth to settings that are conducive to understanding themselves and their faith in new ways is a true advantage. It would be impossible to lead an intimate, soul-searching conversation by the lakeside with a large group. With a single-digit group, you can explore what it might have been like to be Jesus' disciples and imagine their attraction to him and his ministry. How would it feel to believe in something or someone so strongly that we would give up all our belongings and families and leave it all behind?

> Then Jesus summoned his twelve disciples and gave them authority over unclean spirits, to cast them out, and to cure every disease and every sickness. These are the names of the twelve apostles: first, Simon, also known as Peter, and his brother Andrew; James son of Zebedee, and his brother John; Philip and Bartholomew; Thomas and Matthew the tax collector; James son of Alphaeus, and Thaddaeus; Simon the Cananean, and Judas Iscariot, the one who betrayed him. (Matthew 10:1-4)

The disciples were sent on a mission to the lost people of Israel, proclaiming the good news that the kingdom of heaven was close at hand. They were given authority to cure the sick, raise the dead, and cast out demons. Jesus explained that this task would not be easy but that the disciples should not give up, even when others persecuted them.

In the same way, we have a mission to continue telling the stories of the good news and invite youth to follow Jesus' example and become disciples today. Through a wide variety of learning experiences, youth can shape their lives to the ways Jesus taught. And just as Jesus gathered his disciples one or two at a time, so can we gather youth. We are called to care for each one, not only those in larger groups.

One Body

> For just as the body is one and has many members, and all the members of the body, though many, are one body, so it is with Christ. (1 Corinthians 12:12)

Each youth in your congregation is a member of the body of Christ. Each one is unique and brings his or her own gifts and talents as part of the body. So why would a church *not* provide for spiritual growth in whatever ways possible in their particular situation?

Youth gravitate toward youth, just as other peer or interest groups seek one another out. With peers youth will best learn social graces, share their faith journeys, and discuss their life stories. This affinity can take place even between two youth. A single-digit youth group can provide intimacy instead of anonymity and quality regardless of quantity. Teens have so much to offer the church and the world and can powerfully influence their surroundings as a community of faith.

Your youth can share the love of Christ by serving God's people, whoever and wherever they are. Your group may or may not be healing the sick and casting out demons, but you can address many needs. Small groups can easily fulfill local service projects in your community or mission trips to other locations.

If fact, mission-trip groups are usually divided into small groups of two to five youth, depending on the type of work and the space and tools available. So if you have two to five youth, you can have the whole group work together. If you have six to nine youth, you may even need to divide them into two or three groups for specific work.

Within the church, as well as in the mission field, individuals can make a world of difference. Sometimes the most important ministry we can offer is the ministry of presence. So just as God is present when two or three gather in the name of the Lord, be present for the youth in your church. Walk beside them as they explore their faith and grow in deeper relationships with God. Lives will be changed.

Youth Need a Youth Group

Church youth groups in general try to provide a safe environment where youth will feel accepted, loved, and valued. Most youth want to feel this way but may not at school, where many youth don't fit in with their peers. They may experience put-downs, teasing, abusive talk, or inappropriate contact. At school or at home they may be ignored, feeling completely alone in a crowded room.

If youth repeatedly have experiences that deflate their sense of self-esteem and cause them to feel alone, unwanted, and unloved, they may withdraw from social contact. Or they may look for contact in places where they will feel accepted, even unsafe places. Youth could just as easily resort to gangs or other destructive groups as they could turn to positive, character-building environments such as churches. An invitation to a youth group could be just the thing they need, especially if they are often left off other invitation lists.

Youth who fit in peer groups more easily can find other strengths in belonging to a youth group. They may pursue an interest or fulfill a leadership role, which may include mentoring another youth who isn't as outgoing. Youth groups give extraverted youth the opportunity to learn new skills and excel in new experiences.

In addition to helping youth learn about themselves, involvement in a youth group helps them explore and discover God as you guide them in their faith journeys. What an awesome opportunity you have to be a part of life-changing experiences with young people! We can offer youth a wonderful gift by helping them discern God's calling for their lives.

Service and mission projects provide excellent ways for youth to join others in serving God. If we expose them to a variety of experiences and talk about service as a way of life, they will likely continue to serve others throughout their lives. At these times of service, youth often feel God's presence and movement in the lives of others. Together we can truly become the hands and feet of God in serving others.

Many youth will find a church youth group to be a place where others truly listen to them and try to understand their thoughts and feelings. Participation in a group like this gives them the support they need to have a voice in the church and perhaps their community and beyond.

In youth group teens continually discover who they are and can safely try on various ways of relating. They may learn to love someone they didn't even like. They may develop friendships they wouldn't have considered in other settings. Youth in such relationships blossom because instead of judging, they accept one another and discover what they have in common or learn to appreciate the diversity.

Although people rarely mention this fact, youth group also gives caring adults an opportunity to learn and grow in their faith. Participation in youth group may help adults feel accepted, just like the youth. Adults should not serve the youth group because they themselves need attention or care, but they often reap those benefits from their participation in the group. I learn something new every time I'm with youth!

In youth group, life-changing discoveries occur, decisions are made, important questions are asked, relationships are formed and nurtured, and God is revealed over and over again. Our involvement in this vital ministry changes our lives too.

Purpose Statement

Some time ago, a group of youth in leadership spent substantial time studying Scripture and discussing the most important aspects of youth involvement in the church. They developed a purpose statement to describe what effective youth ministry needs to accomplish, and I offer it to you for your consideration in working with youth:

> "The purpose of youth ministry is to provide communities of belonging, through which youth can explore and affirm who they are as gifted people of God and actively live out their Christian faith within the body of Christ and all of God's creation."

The purpose of youth ministry is to provide communities of belonging, through which youth can explore and affirm who they are as gifted people of God and actively live out their Christian faith within the body of Christ and all of God's creation.

Having a purpose statement may be useful both for interpretation of youth ministry to your congregation, and as a guideline to evaluate decisions related to program lessons and activities. If choices of activities don't "measure up" to your statement, choose activities more in line with the stated purpose. You may adopt this statement, adapt it as needed, or create a completely different one, but I encourage you to determine the purpose of your ministry and find a way to interpret that purpose both with the youth and with those who support their faith journeys.

In Ephesians 2:19-22, Paul says:

> You are no longer foreigners and aliens, but fellow citizens with God's people and members of God's household, built on the foundation of the apostles and prophets, with Christ Jesus himself as the chief cornerstone. In him the whole building is joined together and rises to become a holy temple in the Lord. And in him you too are being built together to become a dwelling in which God lives by his Spirit. (NIV)

God intends for us to be in relationship not only with God but also with one another. For teenagers, we can provide a safe place for those relationships to grow in Christ through the church.

Benefits of a Single-Digit Youth Group

Fewer Than Ten Teens: The Good Stuff

Single-digit youth groups have some true advantages. When I formed the youth group I currently work with, we combined youth from four nearby churches. There were only four youth, two of whom were brothers; the other two were girls who were best friends. Having so few didn't bother us, because we were a new youth group and could do things together. The benefits of being a youth group outweighed our concerns about being few in number. Here are some of the discoveries we have made:

Never Too Small to Start

Youth in churches with few teenagers can still participate in a youth group. Some congregations may not have had a youth group for a long time, if ever, so they may greet the potential birth of a group with excitement and hope. Pastors and volunteers in churches with few youth can build a new youth program. When starting a new group where there has not been a youth group in recent years, leaders have a huge advantage in sculpting the group. They'll have little history, if any, with a youth group, so they won't get the "we've always done it this other way" responses. Also, the youth may be happy to have a place to belong and may develop great loyalty to their group. They can be taught the values of making commitments and the discipline of coming to meet with the group every time, regardless of what activity is on the schedule. They'll begin to come because they want to be there and don't want to miss anything.

Influential Faith-Filled Relationships

Youth and adults can benefit from creating strong relationships within the faith. Having access to youth in an organized setting requires only an hour or two a week. However, the time with them through the years can have immense influence. And for some teens, youth group may be the only place they receive affirmation and encouragement. (See Greg's Story.)

Greg's Story

A few years ago I conducted an activity with my youth group where the youth each drew a timeline that started at their birth and ended with the current day. I asked them to draw lines at the approximate times in their lives when significant events happened or special memories were created. One ninth grade boy, Greg, sat staring at his paper with one long line drawn across it and no other marks. The others in the group were working away, but Greg just sat silently.

I managed to maneuver my way to sit beside him and began to ask him questions in hopes that I might stir some ideas for him to use. Yet he just shook his head no as none of my questions were raising anything significant for him. After a few more questions he suddenly turned to me and smiled, saying, "Now I remember something!" He went on to say that he didn't know how to write it, so I asked him to just tell me about it. I was ready to hear something really exciting or unique. He said, "When I was in the fifth grade my teacher, Mrs. Jacobs, was real nice to me." Then he stopped talking. I sat quietly waiting for him to go on with his story. But he turned and looked at me and asked, "So how do I put that on my timeline?"

I was stunned by what he had told me and my heart ached for this young man for whom a teacher's kindness was a significant experience. Hadn't there been hundreds or thousands of other times when people were nice to him? As I tried to think of something to say that would be helpful, he started to speak again. "And now I have my own youth group. Can I put that on my timeline too?" he asked with a huge smile.

By then a couple of youth sitting across from him were picking up on the conversation and began helping him think of other times he could identify as significant events in his life. When Greg was satisfied with what he had on his timeline, he suggested we put all of the timelines on the wall and tape them together to show that we were connected. At that moment I knew we had truly become a group with an identity and a common purpose. So we closed our activity by writing a thank-you letter to God for what we had discovered and shared.

Having heard Greg's story, I don't assume that the lives of my youth are just as they seem. And I haven't forgotten that something as simple as being nice to someone may share a piece of God with others. It didn't matter that our group had only four youth. Youth group was exactly where we needed to be.

Deep and Meaningful Relationships

A small youth group's size allows for relationships to grow faster and deeper, as they could not in a large group. In a single-digit group every teen will usually know the other youth quite well. If they get along, they will attain a high level of trust and have deeper discussions. Their conversations will include their likes, dislikes, dreams, fears, thoughts, and questions about their faith, family situations, and so on. This small group may be the only place they feel comfortable with confiding in others.

Significant Non-Parent Relationships With Youth

The adults often have a major impact on the lives of the youth, forming strong, healthy relationships with them. You will learn about their schools, families, friends, and dreams. Youth often call upon their leaders to write recommendations, serve as references, attend award ceremonies, celebrate rites of passage, and so forth. Some people maintain contact with their leaders for many years after moving on from youth group.

Leadership Potential

All youth can help with the leadership of a single-digit youth group. It's a safe place to try out new skills including how to work with a group. Youth can assist with tasks such as reading the Scriptures, leading devotions, telling stories, and much more. Some youth lead in the forefront, while others help behind the scenes. Both of these leadership styles are valuable and important. You can help each youth develop additional leadership skills and grow stronger in their preferred style.

Many of the leadership skills we try to teach them are actually life skills. For example, learning how to give clear and accurate instructions for a game prepares youth for many kinds of tasks. Reading discussion questions and leading others in a conversation also teaches them skills they can use over time.

Wider Opportunities

Some youth will show exceptional capacity for organizing and leading. The adults working with the youth group may help the youth see their potential and find doors to open for them. Some may want to serve on a team that leads presbytery, district, or conference events and provides them another community of belonging. Others may try leadership at the jurisdictional, national, or even global levels. For leadership roles beyond the local church, youth in single-digit youth groups can have the same opportunity as a youth from a larger group. A large number of youth in a group tends to bring automatic excitement. But teens in small youth groups can have the best of both worlds if we find ways for them to have large-group experiences as a supplement to their youth group. These connections greatly expand their circle of relationships within the church.

> For leadership roles beyond the local church, youth in single-digit youth groups have the same opportunity as youth from a larger group.

Administration

Creating a new program or keeping a single-digit youth group going requires less work than administering a large group. Many of the same tasks need to be done but don't take as long with only a handful of youth. E-mailing, sending postcard reminders, or calling your whole group takes only minutes.

Logistics

You can load a group of fewer than ten youth into one or two vehicles for off-site activities. You don't have to spend a lot of time recruiting drivers or pay gas costs for additional vehicles. A single-digit youth group can also fit into one elevator. You don't have to wait for multiple elevators and struggle to keep your group together. The small number also allows for more spur-of-the-moment outings (assuming you have proper permission and medical authorization forms on file). See the activities in Chapter 7 for ideas that take advantage of this feature of a small youth group.

Church Community

Churches with only a few teens often include their youth in the whole life of the church. Adults may ask teens to usher, sing, garden, read liturgy, teach children's Sunday school, cook, and so forth. To facilitate this inclusion for your youth, you and other adults will need to advocate it among church leaders.

Expenses

Obtaining and maintaining supplies for youth programs and activities costs less than supplies for large groups, especially when buying "per-person" quantities. Getting small donations of items or money to purchase supplies should be easy.

Faith Development

Helping teens explore their faith can be more intentional and extensive in a single-digit youth group. To make church youth group different from other school or community groups, consistently include Bible study and devotional time in your program. You can conduct these activities in less time than you could with a larger group and still maintain high quality. You may even be able to provide individualized Bible study plans or tutoring sessions.

Stealthability

A single-digit youth group can go out in public without being noticed. No large group can claim that advantage! You can do activities a larger group can't do without drawing attention to yourselves, such as a scavenger hunt in a local mall or an outing to a movie theater without having to reserve a large block of seats.

Quick Changes

When you need to change the format of the gatherings, you can quickly tailor it the specific group. You don't have to factor in transition times to move from one activity to another. If you discover a sudden need or situation, you can respond almost instantly. If a program you prepared isn't going smoothly, you can move on to a different one or add a game or music without advance preparation.

Consistency

In a single-digit youth group, no one is anonymous. Everyone in the group knows and notices when one of their group members is missing. Consequently, the same youth tend to return year after year and stay in the program longer when they know they make a difference to the group.

Belonging

Youth who may not fit in with the average social crowd at school can fit into a church youth group and be accepted as an equal. Of course, we would hope a youth group of any size would accept these adolescents. But larger groups tend to divide into cliques, leaving some youth out. A single-digit youth group can intentionally try to include and accept every person in the group. Belonging to a group, even a small one, can boost the self-esteem of youth who are not often included or invited into other groups. Some youth have difficulty becoming part of a group at the risk of being, or at least feeling, rejected.

Commitment

If the group experiences are meaningful and fun and each youth gets attention from the adults and the other youth, as they often do in small groups, the teens will come to meetings regardless of what's on the agenda for that session. Committed to the group, they will not see it as just a place to go if they have nothing better to do. When the youth show up this consistently, the adults will have an easier time staying motivated and interested. Traditionally, youth have attended less frequently as they get older, starting their junior year. By their senior year they show up only occasionally or have dropped out altogether. However, older youth tend to participate in their single-digit youth group through their senior year, because the group has become an important part of their lives.

Growth

One fun factor about having a smaller youth group is that each time you get a new participant, he or she creates a higher percentage of growth! Even if there aren't any more youth in the church to draw from, the youth may have friends visit. Some of those friends may return and become a part of the group in their own right. If they are not already part of a youth group, it's easy to nurture them into your group. If they attend a large church with a larger youth program, they may choose to stay because the size of your group fits their needs, interests, or style.

Events Beyond the Local Church

The small youth group can attend district, conference, presbytery, or regional events along with other teens. Doing so helps them develop ties with youth beyond the local church. These events also build excitement for the youth who attend, so that they return home with new determination and energy. If they relay that story to their congregation, imagine what a lift that news could give their church.

Our mission trip was an example of one of our create-your-own-mission events. My youth decided they wanted to go to the beach. I took them to the coast of northern Oregon, since I wanted to stay reasonably close to home to keep costs to a minimum. We spent two days cleaning up the beach and finding a huge amount of litter.

The third day we went further north to Astoria and worked in a food-bank warehouse that serves twelve helping agencies in that area. We did chores such as sorting apples, moving boxes and piles, and sweeping and hosing down paint scrapings to prepare the building for new paint.

The fourth day we worked at our largest church camp, Camp Magruder. We shoveled and hauled sand and needles from the trees and put them on a trail that needed to be built up to cover exposed roots, which were dangerous. During that cold and windy day, the hard rain soaked us through all layers of clothing. We found the work not much fun but satisfying nonetheless.

The last day, we returned to Portland and worked in our youth center, sorting and organizing supplies and remodeling our kitchen. We tore out some cabinets, painted the whole room, prepared the floor, and put down new flooring.

This great week included hard work, play, laughter, and meaningful discussion and devotion times. And the kids were wonderful: Each youth was included in every activity without any prompting on my part, and the next day six of them came to the youth center to continue the sorting and cleaning, even though they had worked all week!

Common Experience

Single-digit youth groups can have a common experience, such as a mission trip, without dividing into a lot of small groups to do the work. This experience usually leads to many conversations later about the tasks the youth did, the people they met, or how that experience helped them feel closer to God.

Gift of Presence

With only a few youth, you can attend their special events such as concerts, games, award ceremonies, and plays, taking part in their celebrations and rites of passage. You can be there in their times of need or crisis, a responsibility that is even more important.

You could even send them weekly affirmations on postcards or e-mails without a major time commitment. Likewise, the youth can participate in one another's special events to share their joys and carry their burdens. The simple gift of presence adds incredible affirmation for the youth.

Fewer Than Ten Teens: The Not-So-Good Stuff

OK, I admit you may have a few obstacles in working with single-digit youth groups. But I assure you that the benefits outweigh the disadvantages. Here are some things to be aware of:

Finding Resources

Many youth resources are written for groups of larger numbers. But look closely: Most are easy to adapt for your use. Don't be afraid to make whatever changes you need to use the ideas and activities with your group. Check out Chapter 7 for some activities specifically written for fewer than ten teens.

Siblings or Rivals

It isn't unusual for single-digit youth groups to have siblings or rivals. If your group does, you will need to work out a specific agreement about how they will treat each other during youth group time. A group covenant will prove especially helpful in creating the agreement. (See pages 64–65.) Then be sure to enforce the covenant you've created with those two youth. Their behaviors can change with practice and time.

Parents as Adult Leaders

Many people believe that parents of the youth should not be youth group leaders. They argue that the group needs to be a place where the youth can feel comfortable to explore not only their faith but how their faith informs the decisions they make in their daily lives. For some youth, doing so may be difficult with a parent there. Others have no problem with parental involvement and may even welcome it. Sometimes the only available adults are the parents of the youth. If both the youth and the parent agree that they can and want to make it work, then the arrangement can be successful.

To try another approach, have one adult leader who is not a parent of any of the youth and also have a parent of a group member be a helper. This way the parent can opt out of some critical discussions if parental presence might hinder the conversation. (See Chapter 6 for safety procedures to incorporate.)

The Right Leader

While a church's youth ministry should not rely upon the charisma, style, age, or personality of the leader, these factors often influence the attendance of youth. Don't feel locked into having only young adults work with youth. Although younger people tend to have more energy, other advantages come with age. It is more important to have quality leadership than popular leadership. So if we provide leaders who truly care about being advocates for youth, their sincerity and efforts can win over the group. Look for and pray for the right persons.

Personalities

If members of the group don't like one another or don't get along well, those personality conflicts can make or break the group's ability to function. Some youth may not be willing to change their relationships with the other person to make it work. But if they are willing to try, they can usually come to some agreement on how they will relate. This conflict often gives the adult an opportunity to turn to Scripture and have the discussion about how to love people we don't even like. Sometimes the situation can improve just by making the decision that it will improve. Other times people simply annoy one another and no amount of practice can change the personalities. If the teens truly want to have a youth group, they will try to make it work, even if it means merely tolerating another person with whom they wouldn't normally choose to spend time. They can still learn to be kind and caring with that person. Personality conflict is probably one of the most difficult obstacles a youth group ever faces.

Overwhelming Youth

If your congregation has only a few youth, the same ones get asked over and over again to do every project or be on every committee. They can easily become overwhelmed by needing to "represent" the youth in too many places. A good session or two on time management might help the youth balance where they volunteer their time within the church.

Attendance

Even if you have eight or nine youth, weak attendance leads to only two or three showing up at group gatherings. Therefore the whole group needs to make a covenant that they will attend as often as possible. If they choose not to live up to that agreement, the group will dwindle. Each youth should expect the others to show up at scheduled gatherings. But remember that if you have only one, two, or three youth, you need not be disappointed. Work with those you have since each one is important. See Chapter 7 for ideas on activities for one or more youth.

A Final Word

Your youth may have friends and schoolmates who attend much larger youth groups in nearby cities or in churches of other denominations. If so, don't compare your group size to others. Instead, spend that energy on making this group's activities as effective as possible and don't be hard on yourself or your group about its size. Own it and be excited about it.

3 Adult Leaders

Back to the Basics

No youth group of any size can exist without adults who are willing to invest in the lives of teenagers. Period. Most leaders of single-digit youth groups are volunteers. They usually come with leadership skills, good intuition, and a passion for the youth but not much experience or training. Adult leaders need to be grounded in the basics, keeping them in mind when working with a youth group, especially a small one.

Set realistic visions and goals.

Your group doesn't need to look just like any other youth group, so work together to identify what the group needs to be. Make some intentional decisions and agreements, then determine how the group can make its vision a reality. Stretch and challenge yourselves, but not to the point where you are likely to fail.

Stay grounded in the Word.

Some youth who attend Sunday school or Bible studies may feel that youth group is just a time to play. While church experiences should be fun, they should also foster learning and growing in community and faith. If the group can stay grounded in what really brings them together, their fun times will become meaningful.

Show that you live your faith.

The teens may or may not completely listen to what you try to teach them, but they will quickly see whether you live what you profess. When we live in the ways Jesus taught, youth will see Christ and the active movement of the Spirit among us. Then it's easy for the youth to have heart-to-heart conversations with you about how their faith informs their decisions and shapes their future. Youth may also learn how to be responsible members of the church from our example. When we attend Sunday school and worship or serve on teams and committees, we invite youth to do the same.

Youth see how you treat others, and they hear what you say to or about other people. If you do your best to embody the fruit of the Spirit, that effort will show in your interactions with your youth and with others. If you show interest in each of the youth, expressing concern or joy at their life experiences, they will remember your kindness. The youth will also notice that you don't gossip, stereotype, or complain about people. Then when you ask them to do the same, they can follow your example.

Affirm your youth.

We don't often know how much our affirmation affects youth. For the teens in healthy family situations, we may be one of several people who remind them of their value, commendable achievements, and importance to others. For teens who don't live in settings where they receive positive affirmation, youth group may be the only place they experience it. This sad situation happens all too often. (See page 81 for the Affirmation Boxes activity).

In a single-digit youth group you have a great opportunity to meet the youth where they are in their social and spiritual development. You will know their activities, their attitudes, and eventually their faith experiences. They will not all be in the same place spiritually, physically, and emotionally, so we can all enjoy the diversity and learn from it.

Guide youth to become disciples.

Youth group is the ideal place for teens to learn and practice spiritual disciplines and pathways to God and to identify the elements in their lives that can become spiritual disciplines or experiences. Help them understand that their schoolmates, neighbors, and fellow church members come in many different forms and that part of following Christ includes learning to love those you don't even like. If teens learn this lesson, their entire adult lives will be richer. What a great gift from God!

Help youth gain and maintain healthy friendships.

If teens feel good about their youth group, they will bring friends. Some will only visit, but others may become part of the group. As a leader of a single-digit youth group, you will know both parties to a friendship. Consequently, you will have the opportunity to help youth learn how to strengthen their friendships, both by teaching specific behaviors and attitudes and by modeling being a friend. You will also be able to support your youth in shifting directions in a friendship if a change for the positive is needed.

Help youth claim youth group as their own.

Some youth may not want to be at youth group. They come because their parents insist. If you have any of these youth, include programs and discussions that will engage their interest. Help them realize that youth group is not only their parents' idea of a good place, but it is a good place they can claim as their own. Be sure they know you're glad they have attended, but don't smother them; help them slowly transition into the youth group. This approach won't work for every youth, but it will work for many.

Help youth discover themselves.

Youth commonly adopt the attitudes of their parents, as well as rebel against being like their parents. Neither of these ends of the spectrum is completely right or wrong, but youth would find a healthier sense of self by striking somewhere in between. In a youth group you have a chance to help youth discover who they are as individuals and identify their own outlook on the situations life presents.

Invite youth to make decisions for their group.

Youth have the ability to decide some of the discussion topics and social activities for the year. Make sure to expose them to important topics and activities, but leave plenty of time for topics of their choice as well. If they choose, they will become more interested in the programs. Don't hesitate to work with them as a team—ask them to help you plan and lead the activities.

You don't have to be an expert.

You don't need to know a lot about every topic, issue, or lifestyle that concerns or interests teens to be a good leader. No one can know everything, so don't discount a topic because you're unfamiliar with it. It's OK to say, "I don't know" or "Let's figure out how we can get that information." Then do some research together. This quest can prove to be a great learning experience.

Enjoy the youth both as a group and as individuals.

Youth are truly amazing, skilled, bright, fun, caring, concerned, hard working, and a whole lot of fun! Don't be so busy planning and leading that you miss the fun!

> Youth are truly amazing, skilled, bright, fun, caring, concerned, hard working, and a whole lot of fun! Don't be so busy planning and leading that you miss the fun!

Learn along with your youth.

One of the wonderful side benefits of working with youth is that you will continue to learn. As you prepare studies, programs, and experiences, you can't help but encounter something new, or see a different approach, or understand in another way. So, the time spent volunteering or working as a youth leader benefits you possibly as much as it benefits the youth.

What Are You Afraid Of?

Taking on responsibilities for a youth group of any size can be daunting. Adults often worry about their abilities to work with youth. Knowing how to address these concerns will make recruiting helpers much easier, whether they are taking on regular leadership or just helping out for a specific occasion. Here are some common fears you and other potential leaders may have:

Will I be accepted?

Youth are not the only ones who have uncertainties about how other people will receive them. We all want to be liked and accepted. It's natural to wonder how well you'll relate to others. The youth are probably wondering if you will like and accept them as well.

Will others challenge my authority or respect me as their leader?

It's difficult to know if group members are ready for a new leader and whether they will give you the benefit of the doubt. You may wonder, "Will they be measuring me against the previous leader? Will they really allow me to become their leader? Will they cooperate with me?"

If you are beginning a new group where everyone is starting together, youth who choose to attend will likely respect you. In many ways, beginning a group from scratch is easier than entering an existing group or restarting a previously existing group. If you're taking on one of these tasks, the history of the group can sometimes become a hurdle. Climb over it as gracefully as you can.

What if I'm too old or too young?

We tend to assume older people don't relate as well to youth as younger adults do. In my experience, youth will accept adults of any age as long as the adults seem comfortable, interested, and helpful. If they show nervousness or don't converse with the youth, they won't connect with the teens, regardless of age. Young adult leaders need to behave as adults and make it evident to the youth that they're not trying to still be teenagers. Some people have no problem filling the leadership role at an early age, while others have difficulty for many years. Leading youth isn't just about age; it's about maturity and appropriate behaviors and attitudes.

What if I'm out of my comfort zone?

It's OK to have to stretch a bit to work with youth. Many of the youth will be feeling the challenge of coming into a new group as well. You will likely become more comfortable as you spend more time with the youth. If you don't find the role of leader easier after a reasonable length of time, you want to reconsider whether or not youth ministry is the area that suits you. But don't give up too quickly. You may just need some time to adjust.

Will others trust and value my influence?

Others will trust you if you are trustworthy. You may need to earn their trust. So be honest and keep confidences when asked to do so. If you participate in rumors or discussion about people not present, others will quickly lose trust in you.

It follows that if others trust you, they will likely accept your influence and come to value your leadership. If they do not trust you, they will not value your influence or even your presence. Sometimes others will convince someone else that you aren't trustworthy. If the problem is truly about something or someone else rather than you, you will need to tread carefully. But again, honesty is the best choice. Initiate conversation. Work to resolve differences and misunderstandings. The effort is worth it.

Do I know enough?

No tests exist that can tell whether you know enough to work with any particular group. To be a youth leader, you do not need to know all about every topic that may come up in the group. You can say, "I don't know." But you can help the group find the information they need to answer their question or study the topic further.

You do have the responsibility of searching for materials and conversations that will keep you up to date on youth issues. Even though you were once a teenager, today's youth culture is significantly different in some ways, and you will benefit your youth and yourself by staying in tune with their lives and influences. You may have a youth or two who are willing to spend some additional time helping you get up to speed. Perhaps you could designate a program time on a present-day topic and have the group teach you.

Do I have enough time or skills?

Only you can say whether you have enough time. You need to choose your priorities and decide to what extent you would like to be involved. You may choose to give less time to other activities for at least a while. Or you may decide that you aren't interested in sacrificing other interests to put more time into youth group. It's completely up to you to decide and make your decision clear to those who invite you to participate. If you don't, you may get swept into more than you bargained for, and it's harder to back out.

After you have committed your time to youth group, you may worry about whether you have the specific skills needed for the job. But hands-on experiences, other adults, and training events can teach you. However, know your limitations. If you have physical restrictions, don't get into the middle of an overactive game where you are likely to get injured.

You won't be as much help to the group if you have to spend time recovering from injuries.

What will be expected of me if I agree to serve in this way?

Ask this question before you make a decision or commitment. The person inviting you to serve should have specific information or be able to refer you to someone who has more details. Youth groups, even single-digit ones, need multiple adults involved with varying levels of commitment. You may have several options from which to select. Full-time leadership is only one way; consistent helper and occasional helper are two others.

What if I make a mistake?

Most people do, sooner or later. No one is perfect, and minor mistakes are bound to happen. You may call a youth by the wrong name, for instance. Just apologize and let him or her know you will be more careful in the future. Then find a special way to remember that person's name. After hearing you say the right name several times, the person will probably forget about the mistake.

If the problem is something more serious, immediately seek assistance from a member of the clergy or another adult. Don't let it fester into something even worse. (See Chapter 6 on safety for specific recommendations.)

> These fears are not only common to youth workers but are shared by many other people in fields unrelated to youth ministry.... You are not alone. The good news is you can overcome most or all of your fears with some effort and the support of others who also feel called to work with youth.

After rereading this list, I realize that these fears are not only common to youth workers but are shared by many other people in fields unrelated to youth ministry. Any person looking for work or new to a job might feel the same way. You are not alone. The good news is you can overcome most or all of your fears with some effort and the support of others who also feel called to work with youth.

Starting or Restarting a Single-Digit Youth Group

If a congregation wants to guide and nurture youth in their faith, then a youth group, no matter how small, has a good possibility of working.

On the other hand, some churches begin youth programs with the hope that having young people active in their congregation will somehow "save" their declining or aging congregation. If the church discusses a youth program for this reason only and does not focus on the youth, it is going the right direction for the wrong reason. Before you begin, be clear about the focus.

This chapter includes practical helps for starting a new group or a cooperative youth group with more than one church. (See Chapter 5 for more specific information about starting a cooperative youth ministry.) If you're restarting or revitalizing an existing youth group, follow the same steps but also evaluate what is needed and what is not.

How to Organize

Begin by inviting all potential youth group members, interested parents, and other adults to meet. Ask both the adults and youth at the meeting what they would like the youth to do and learn in youth group. Use these questions to guide your conversation and begin shaping your youth ministry plan:

- What are the greatest needs of the youth in our congregation and community?
- Which of those needs do we feel our church will be able to respond to?
- What specific goals or accomplishments will this ministry achieve?
- What difficulties or obstacles could get in the way of these goals?
- What resources does our church have to help this ministry be successful?
- Who are the people in our congregation who truly care about youth?
- What other questions have come to mind at this point?

Next, identify adults in the congregation who might take on some responsibility for leading the youth group. Who are the adults in your congregation who may be willing to spend time with youth on a regular basis? (These adults may or may not be present in the first meeting.) Ask the youth what adults they would like to see in youth group. Then invite those adults to meet with you to discuss your vision, and solicit their support for the new program.

Be sure to indicate a specific time limit you are asking adults to serve. Let them know this arrangement will be reviewed at least annually, if not more often, to allow them to agree to continue or not continue, or to change their role in the program, guilt-free. But emphasize the importance of continuity and consistency in the lives of the youth.

If the church, or group of churches, intends to create a paid position, be clear about the expectations and compensation you are able and willing to offer. Consider developing a job description. The book *10 Things I Wish I'd Known When I Started in Youth Ministry*, by Reuellyn Pletcher, (Abingdon Press, 2004) offers excellent help in this area. If you are a part of a connectional denomination, contact your presbytery, district, or conference to make them aware of the job opening. They may know persons who are potential candidates.

Once your adult leadership is in place, invite the youth to meet with the adults to determine what type of program may work best in your congregation's setting. You may want to begin by reviewing the purpose statement of youth ministry on page 14 to kick off a conversation. Or create your own version for discussion. This statement provides a guideline to work with and a tool to interpret youth ministry to your congregation. It's hard to build something when you don't know what you want it to look like. So take the necessary time to complete this step, which will define the steps that come next.

Then craft the group's ideas into a plan for the first three months. (See page 34 for some sample meeting formats.) Stick with that plan and then evaluate it at the end of the three months. At that point you can adjust that plan to incorporate more ideas or start a new plan that would work better for the group. Continue to plan and to evaluate, learning from your experiences. Be patient with the plan and with one another. All too often, the youth leaders or the congregation give up on the youth program before it has had time to become well established and stable. Good things can take time to develop, so allow the time and do the job well.

Where to Meet

Examine the options available for the group's meeting space. Consider the potential size of the group and include some extra room in case the ministry grows. Ideally, the youth would have a room or cluster of rooms that can be dedicated to their group. It's best not to need to share the space with other groups or meetings. The room can be made much more comfortable if the youth can put up decorations and lighting; leave out art projects to dry;

have a stereo system; and post charts, topical study sheets, and photos from activities without having to take them down or put everything away or behind locked closet doors every time they leave.

Another consideration is having space that is not next to a typically quiet area, such as a chapel or sanctuary, or the pastor's study or office. Teenagers, and even their group leaders, need to be loud sometimes.

If the group is from several churches, you may have more than one space to consider. However, be aware of the dynamics that can come into play if a newly combined group decides to meet in a room that is already a youth space or classroom at one church. No matter how hard you try to make it "new space," the youth from that church will feel it is "their" space. The youth not from that church will feel like visitors instead of group members.

This dynamic is very hard to overcome, so don't take it too lightly. The best space would be a room or two not already used as youth space. Then the group can start from scratch to make it their own. If you must use an existing youth space, then move the furniture and redecorate, so that you start with a fresh look created by the new group.

If a church room is not available, scout out other meeting spaces. They may not provide the luxury of decorating and such, but they will at least allow the group to meet consistently. Maybe someone has a basement room in his or her house, or maybe there's a neighborhood community center. Perhaps there is an RV or trailer in a church member's driveway. You may need to get creative, but don't give up. Youth adapt easily. In some ways, the stranger the situation, the more they rise to the occasion and get interested in the novelty of it.

We Did It This Way: Creating Our Space

When I began with four youth in a cooperative ministry setting, we had obstacles to overcome, but doing so became a part of the building the group. To have a long-term youth ministry, the churches had decided to hire me as a part-time director. One church had difficulty securing their share of the funding for the director but gladly provided part of their huge building for dedicated youth space.

Luckily, I went in a few days before the first orientation meeting to see the space and setup. The room, an old gymnasium, had become a storage area for broken or extra furniture through the years. The floor was breaking up, and the ceiling was breaking down! The water heating pipes were disconnected and lying on the floor. Although the space had great potential, we couldn't use it unless we did some work. I started to feel hopeless.

We scheduled the orientation meeting for a different room and included the youth, their parents, the pastors, and a few interested adults. I came with a schedule of days and times I could be there to work with anyone willing to help fix up the room, and I invited them to sign up for work shifts. Our youth group started by repairing our new space. We made a list of supplies and put a notice in the church mailings and bulletins requesting donations, which started pouring in.

By the end of six months, we had repaired the ceiling, gotten the church trustees to repair the heating, painted the room, acquired furniture and basic supplies, and had new carpeting installed. We did it all without the group actually having any money. The day the carpet was installed, we did an overnight and slept on our new carpet. Working together for a common goal was a great way to get to know one another. We were then ready to make our plan for the next stages and move forward. It wasn't hopeless after all.

When to Meet

Once you've made a plan, begin holding weekly gatherings. I decided early on to hold a youth group meeting every week, even if only one youth showed up. I arrived each week with a back-up plan of how to adapt that week's activity to one, two, or three kids. I tried to be sure they didn't read disappointment on my face instead of the joy of seeing those who were there. If no youth came, I used that time to write postcards to the youth, telling them I missed them and reminding them of the next meeting and activity. I was persistent, if not annoyingly nagging. But they needed to know that each of them was important and that their absences affected the other members of the group.

Weekly meetings often do not provide enough time for consistency and the chance to enjoy being together. But trying to meet more often may conflict with after-school activities. At the other extreme, meeting less than once a week makes it difficult to have continuity and feel connected.

I have a policy of not asking my youth to do more than one activity per weekend. My group meets Sunday evenings for ninety minutes unless we have a special activity such as a service project or a district or regional youth event. If we meet Friday or Saturday for an activity, we will not meet on Sunday night of that weekend. This practice allows families to have time together on a weekend, does not overload the youth leader, and gives us the chance to be together without getting tired of one another. We also make exceptions during Christmas and other church seasons. Since the youth group doesn't overwhelm their family schedules, the parents don't resent the time the youth spend at church.

The right day or night of the week to meet is completely up to the group and the adult leaders. You might want to make a chart showing each person and each day of the week. Then put in symbols for the days they would each prefer and the days they know they won't be available. After you eliminate some days, you can decide among the remaining options.

One thing I like about Sunday evening is that we can meet 5:30–7:00 P.M., the usual dinner time. The youth have all of Sunday afternoon for family time, and they still have the rest of the evening after youth group to do the homework they haven't done yet.

I rarely accept homework woes as a good excuse to miss youth group. Teens need to learn how to manage their time, and fitting in both youth group and homework is part of that learning experience. I'm only asking for an hour and a half out of their entire weekend, so I expect them to adjust if at all possible. I do understand, though, that some events are clearly beyond their control. The week before final exams, we may do an evening of "study hall" at the youth room. The youth can continue to study and still have

We Did It This Way: No Previews

At first the youth would ask what we were going to be doing the next week. I intentionally answered in a vague manner but always assured them the program would be fun and worth their time. Before long they stopped asking and just kept coming.

This change felt like a huge accomplishment on my part. I had never had a group before who would just come because they wanted to be there. What a treat to not feel that I was twisting arms every week or that they would come only if they didn't get a better offer from someone else. I could then put my energy into other elements of the program.

friends to visit. Those without homework can play a table game, read a good book, or draw—anything appropriate and low key.

Whatever the situation, my youth know I want them to be there; I'm not ambivalent about their attendance. I don't know about you, but when persons make it clear that they want to spend time with me, I can usually find a way to fit that meeting into my schedule.

Inviting Youth

Do some research through the church office about the congregation's families to discover who all of the potential youth are. Some youth may even attend on their own or with a friend. While you may have difficulty gaining the interest and trust of older youth when beginning a new group, it can't hurt to at least let them know they're invited and welcome.

I like to label the first two weeks of a new youth group "try it out" weeks. This label takes some of the pressure off the youth. If they think that showing up to any meeting means making a commitment, they might hesitate to come. I'd prefer that they come a few times and then make an intentional decision to continue or gracefully stop. When a youth decides to stop attending, both you and the youth will feel better about the decision in the long run, and he or she might even come again later.

Another approach is to learn something about each of the youth you are going to invite (such as places they've been, favorite activities, movies, or video games, and so forth). Include references to some of those preferences on the invitation. It might surprise them and catch their interest.

Be sure they know they may bring a friend. Youth who are quiet or shy might have a difficult time just coming on their own but may feel more comfortable when bringing a friend. You could even enclose a second invitation for them to give to their friend.

Once the group has started meeting, have them think of more ways to invite other youth to the group. You may ask them to invite youth from the original list whom they don't know, or you may ask them to recruit teens in their neighborhoods. Talk with your pastor or evangelism committee for ideas about how to invite people you don't know. Maybe you can combine efforts and invite whole families from a certain neighborhood.

Meeting Formats

Youth group meetings come in a variety of formats, so choose the best one for your particular group. Remember that your ministry's goal is to help youth grow in their faith and not to simply entertain them. Spiritual development can happen in many different settings while remaining fun and interesting. Here are some sample formats to help you think through your group's options:

- Traditional format, which blends elements almost every week: gathering, game, Scripture, activity, refreshments, devotions, closing circle with prayer and benediction
- Monthly rotation of elements, with one of the following per week: Bible study, topic program, recreation, service project, worship, meal, games
- Monthly focus on one element or interest area
- Monthly focus on one topic, but various styles
- Any monthly pattern with a special event, project, or retreat for every fifth Sunday
- Bible study every week
- Servant team that either does a project, prepares for a project, or learns about a project or agency each week
- Youth choir or praise band with devotions or Bible study
- Reflection or discussion group that responds to movies, songs, current events, art, speakers, stories, drama, humor, or study books
- Discussion group that holds personal conversations about life and faith
- Drama or comedy group that writes and performs skits or plays about Christian topics
- Writing group that writes in journals or composes poetry, stories, and liturgy
- Media group that deals with videos, computers, video games, music, and news
- Art group that uses art as a spiritual discipline, creating collages, mosaics, paintings, candles, cards, banners, journals, photos, sculptures, and so forth (These could be self-funded through sales of created items.)

Work as a group to determine the interests, learning styles, and schedule that will best fit the group. Be creative and do what the group is excited about. Learning and growing as disciples can happen in many different ways, so be adaptable.

Meaningful Rituals

While the format and even the content for your meetings may change, youth see consistent rituals as important. Build some in. A ritual can be as simple as opening with prayer and Scripture reading or ending with prayer and a benediction.

I have used a traditional and popular benediction that is based on Numbers 6:24-26. It reads:

> May the Lord bless you and keep you. May the Lord make his face to shine upon you and be gracious unto you. May the Lord lift up his countenance upon you and give you peace. Amen.

Another short one goes like this:

> May God, who teaches us to reach out to others, continue to remind us to be caring in this group and at home with our families. May God be with us while we're apart this week and bring us safely back together in celebration of your love. Amen.

The youth group can write their own benediction as well.

Group Covenant

After trying many different ways of building a youth group, I have found creating a group covenant highly effective. This procedure allows the full youth group to agree on guidelines by which it will monitor itself throughout the year.

Together the youth read and discuss Scripture passages that teach us how we should treat others. Then they decide what behaviors and practices will make their group time the best possible experience, and they write statements describing these elements for the group to review. Once the group members review and edit the statements, they finalize the list.

I like to have each person in the group (both the youth and the adults) sign the covenant as a commitment to the other group members. Each person agrees to abide by the covenant as much as possible. When the group members have made the covenant clear, it can help them monitor their behavior and remember what the group is about.

Post the covenant on the wall in the meeting space for all to see. Having your covenant visible in a room that is also used by other groups shows what the youth group feel is important about their time together, which serves as a good model for others.

To read the process for developing a covenant and a sample covenant, turn to pages 64 and 65. Be creative and adapt it to your group.

We Did It This Way: Creating a Ritual

I put the words of the benediction on a large poster. At first we read it each week. Before long the youth found it pretty easy to remember the three phrases and had it memorized. But I've left the poster on the wall so that any visitor or parent picking up a teen may participate in the closing prayer without having to know the benediction from memory.

Good Resources

Ask your pastor or education committee where to buy curriculum resources. Don't assume you are on your own and have to come up with all of the programming. Good materials are available. (See the list on page 112 for some recommendations.) Remember to ask if the church already owns any print or media materials for youth groups.

Whether you choose new or reclaimed resources, review them and make notes about possible uses. Remember that since curriculum resources are written for churches all across the country, you will want to adapt them to fit your particular group. Nowadays curriculum resources commonly include a variety of program and Bible study options from which to choose. Also, Chapter 7 of this book give you a variety of activities specifically for fewer than ten teens.

Among the best resources are other youth leaders. They have experience and wisdom to share and perhaps materials they are willing to loan. People to turn to can make your work much easier and less lonely. Be sure to take advantage of training opportunities offered by your denomination. The workshops are helpful, and the event is an opportunity to meet and network with other youth workers.

Congregational Support

Youth group should be a ministry of the whole church, not just a few interested adults with the youth. Look for ways to relate the youth to the congregation and to help the congregation learn about the youth group. Have the teens participate in some activities with other church members.

However, try not to give into the urge to "show off" the youth or "use" the youth. It's a fine line between offering the youth opportunities to participate

and serve, and parading them in front of the adults so that the adults will feel good about having young people in the church. Why are youth often the first to be asked to serve a dinner, do the dishes, assist an adult with childcare, pull weeds, rake leaves, and so forth? Sometimes youth are the only ones who are physically able to do those jobs in a congregation of many older adults. However, the youth often feel that the adults don't want to do those jobs themselves and assume the youth somehow owe the church their services. Be careful not to let the youth be used or abused. Make sure they are invited or asked to do jobs and given a reason why they should take on those tasks. Then let them agree—or not.

An effective way to involve other church members in the life of the youth group is to ask for their prayers. Keep them up to date about the group's programs, service projects, and study topics. Then ask the congregation to support the group with their prayers, which doesn't cost them a thing.

Later, when you ask the church members to support the group financially, they will perhaps be more open to hearing about the needs of the group. Always be up front and clear about why the group needs funding and how the money will be spent. People will often rise to the occasion to support a youth project even if they don't give to a building campaign or other projects. Give them the opportunity to support the group.

Family Support

Although we may sometimes feel as though we are exclusively in ministry with youth, we are not. They certainly are our priority, but their families are next in line. What we do and discuss in youth group may affect the families of our youth. On the other hand, we are not the only ones concerned with the spiritual lives of the youth. Many families are also. We are not alone; we have strong allies among at least some of the parents, if not all.

Keep parents informed and get their support for the program. When I send the youth a mailing with the group schedule and other information, I also send a separate copy to their parents. I want to later be able to ask the parents to get their kids to youth group and on time. They can't do so if they don't know the schedule. And you can't always rely on the youth to give their parents copies of what you send home or even mail home. Sometimes it happens, but more often not.

> ### We Did It This Way: Communicating With Youth and Parents
>
> I have found that one easy way to send reminders out to the youth is by a large postcard on bright colored paper. It will be noticeable in their pile of mail, and if the parents happen to sort the mail first, they will have an opportunity to see the announcement or reminder without actually "opening" someone else's mail. This method works pretty well, since the youth tend to forget to deliver the information to their parents.

Once you get to know the parents a bit, talk with them about how the youth group schedule and their family schedule fit together. Ask parents not to plan family activities during youth group sessions, which take up only small amount of time out of their week. Assure the parents that you will give them advance notice of any youth group activities set at times other than the usual youth group meeting time.

Church Staff Support

The pastor and any other staff can make a big difference in how well the congregation accepts and includes the youth group. If they support the group and its endeavors, they can positively influence the congregation. A lack of support will not help the congregation care for the group. So try to keep the pastor and staff informed. If you are the pastor and are serving as the youth leader, keep the congregation informed. Plenty of information is better than people either wondering or not even noticing what the youth are doing. Be sure to meet deadlines for submitting information to a church newsletter or bulletin.

Prayer Support

Pray continuously for the youth in your congregation and community. We offer youth one of the best gifts we have when we pray for them. On page 107 you will find a prayer worksheet to help you identify people you want to pray for. You can also use it as a tool for teaching youth how to pray. At the closing time of each group gathering, have a share-and-prayer circle where the youth can mention joys and concerns and request prayers. (You can use the worksheet as a guide to what to include in some of those prayer times.) If you conduct the prayer circle week after week and month after month, the youth will become comfortable with the routine and learn to pray with you or on their own.

Holding a prayer-a-thon creates a fun yet meaningful activity (see page 88–90). You might also have each youth have a prayer partner for whom they pray each day. You can change partners weekly, monthly, or as often as you like.

Long-Term View

Do not be discouraged by small numbers. The number of attendees, especially when beginning a new program, does not measure the quality of the program. It's too soon to know whether the the quality of the program is good or bad. Resist the pressure, whether from yourself or others, to struggle for bigger numbers in order to prove "success."

You may well need to "grow" your own youth program. Looking at the long term, begin with activities for younger age levels (fourth through sixth grade) while preparing for them as young teens. (*Tween Time* and *Tween Time 2* provide activities for older elementary school children; see Resources on page 112.) This approach can take several years and requires persistence, but building a community of youth is well worth the effort.

We Did It This Way: Building for the Future

With my cooperative youth group, we have a group for grades four through six and another group for grades seven through twelve. They both meet weekly, at the same time, and in the same building. Both groups meet together four times a year for a meal or activity. The younger ones know that they will automatically move on to the older group when they complete sixth grade. Meeting this way serves as a terrific ministry and provides a feeder group to the older youth group. Some families have youth in both groups, so our matching time and location benefits them as well. (See Chapter 5 for more about cooperative ministry.)

Cooperative Youth Ministry

"What can we do together that we can't do apart?"
"What can we do more effectively together than apart?"

These questions drive the search for partners in ministry. Churches with only a few youth often do not think they have any viable way of providing a youth group, but a cooperative youth ministry can serve well. Two or more churches or groups can join their resources, including the necessary adults, to create an effective youth ministry.

With a passion for young people and for youth ministry, I have worked successfully in several churches. But nearly ten years ago, I lost a full-time youth ministry staff position because of budget cuts. The loss turned into opportunity. I met with a group of churches who really wanted to have a youth program. They envisioned combining their efforts to provide one program for four churches. I decided to take their offer to help make that dream happen.

Start-Up Issues and Assumptions

Talking through the viability of such a plan, we identified our immediate issues and assumptions about potential obstacles:

They needed a start-up grant in order to hire a youth director with enough experience to create a youth program from scratch with churches who hadn't had successful youth programs for many years. Then each of the four churches would need to share the monthly costs. Others told us this arrangement would not work. Financing the program has indeed been a challenge when money has been tight, but the churches have shown dedication toward our group. One church in particular has a limited ability to provide adults or money, but it provides meeting space for both groups.

Some feared that the youth involved in the program might not participate in their own local churches on Sunday mornings because they would be trying to get together with the youth from other churches. That situation has not happened. The youth have remained active in their own congregations for everything except youth group.

They expected that finding adults from various churches willing to help the program would be hard. This situation has also not happened; we have seven adults each week (two leaders and five helpers).

Our Story

The group I currently work with began with four churches offerings one cooperative program. We started with four youth. From one church came two brothers, and from a second church came two girls who were best friends. The other two churches didn't have any youth but hoped that if they were part of the cooperative group they could offer a youth program if ever youth came to their church or as younger children grew into the ages to be included in the youth program.

We have been together for nine years. Sometimes one or two youth would show up for youth group, but we just kept meeting. They knew I would be there every week no matter what. Before long, they attended every week too.

We have a group of fourth through sixth graders and a group of seventh through twelfth graders who meet at the same time, in the same building, and in neighboring rooms. We fluctuate from year to year with numbers of youth, but the group is solid, with seven adults attending weekly between the two groups.

The numbers don't really matter; our decision to work together has made all the difference. We started when we only had a few youth and just stayed with the ministry through the years.

Continuing Hurdles

Some hurdles always seem to be out there ahead of us:

Funding is always an issue. Most of these congregations are small and struggle to maintain their building, let alone pay for staff. Even the clergy work only part time in some of them. Decaying buildings, declining participation by young families, economic stresses, and aging congregations make cooperative ministry difficult.

It's hard to track the schedules of several churches and find time with youth that does not occasionally overlap with the times for other events in at least one church. Even though the churches try to work around the regular youth group meeting time, they sometimes have difficulty finding ways to do so.

Organization and communication become more complex. Who keeps track of what? Who's in charge of what? When and where will the Steering Committee meet, and who will lead it? How do we divide the financial responsibilities? How will we supervise and coordinate with the church staff? Who will take notes and distribute them, along with meeting notices, to the members? You get the picture. Not having the answers makes doing nothing easier. But such an attitude won't keep a program functioning.

The youth have to do more than their share of the fundraising to remain afloat. The churches can barely manage the salary support let alone program expenses.

Definite Advantages

The hurdles of cooperative youth ministry may seem like big problems. However, the advantages outnumber those issues in our experience:

1. We provide a program where none existed for a long time.

2. We provide a program for the expanded age range. The younger group also serves as a feeder group to the junior high, so that its members automatically enter youth group when they reach seventh grade.

3. The youth in the group experience community within diversity. Coming from different churches (and some from no church), they attend different schools. Their hobbies include athletics, computers, reading, ballet, playing an instrument, composing, writing, student leading, art, social activism, mechanics, construction building, cooking, and other activities.

4. They come because they want a Christian community of belonging and faith experiences.

5. They invite friends because they want to share what they have: acceptance and the assurance that God is with us.

6. Invited friends often become full members on their own, regardless of the friendship that originally brought them to the group. Some of these youth even attend churches of other denominations or areas of the city (or they may have no church at all). But they belong to the youth group, which does not focus on these differences.

7. Sometimes non-church parents or other family members begin to participate in local churches.

8. The youth feel as though they all make up the group and are not just visitors in someone else's church. This perception boosts the group's morale. It also helps those who attend churches of other denominations or areas, or no church at all, feel accepted instead of feeling like strays or visitors. The youth make a big effort to welcome and include additional people. They take them in right at the first visit, and treat them like family.

9. The youth have their own place. They meet in one of the local churches where we have been provided a space for just this group. They can decorate their own room, feeling a part of a unique group. The space is also available any time we want to offer a supplemental activity, training, counseling, prayer group, or meetings. The other churches in the cooperative ministry let us use their facilities as well.

10. The youth group makes the decisions about activities and schedules. It's small enough that the whole group can participate instead of having to form a smaller core team. This ability gives them ownership of the group as well as a great way to learn and safely practice Christian leadership skills. Several of my youth have even led our group successfully when I have been out of town.

11. The group consistently meets every week, same time, same place, with exceptions only for special events away from the church or the occasional lock-in or work project. Some youth who attend on alternate weeks because of visits to family members can still expect us to be there when they come. This consistency also helps set a habit of going to church each week. Church and youth group can be some of the most consistent positive factors in teens' lives.

12. E-mail helps the group keep in touch with one another. The youth use it to request prayers and connect in ways they haven't before.

Is Cooperative Youth Ministry for You?

Individual churches must find their own ways to maintain or revitalize their ministries. Don't be afraid to try new things or old things in new ways. If we always do the same things in the same ways the results will always be the same. That reluctance to change won't move us forward.

Is cooperative youth ministry for you? See the questions below, which will guide discussion in determining your church's answer to this question. But before you even look at them, spend time in prayer and listen for God's guidance. When the time comes for discussion, begin with prayer to help the group better focus and feel the nudges God may be giving them one way or the other.

Partnering with other churches isn't the answer for every church, but it presents an option worth pursuing. I think cooperative ministry will become more and more common as we look for new ways to reach out to youth and help lead them to a deeper faith.

◦

Here are some questions to consider in determining whether a cooperative ministry might benefit your congregation's youth ministry or youth group:

• Are we lacking something we would like help obtaining? (for example, a youth group, a youth leader, an organized program, more youth, program development, print resources)

• Could some of what we lack be improved by joining with another youth group or multiple groups? (for example, increase in numbers, experienced leadership, resources)

• What would the youth in our congregation like to do that isn't happening? (for example, mission trips, recreation, Bible Study)

• Are our youth willing to wholeheartedly accept other youth as part of their group? (If the youth aren't willing, no kind of program or leadership will work.)

• What do we have to offer a grouping of multiple-church youth groups? (for example, interested youth, leader, meeting space)

• What would we be asking them to do or provide? (for example, leader, funding, resources, meeting space)

• Would our youth be willing to meet in a designated space in a different church building?

• Are we willing to consider a multi-denominational (as well as multi-congregational) youth group?

• What else do we need to know to make a decision about pursuing cooperative ministry options?

> If we always do the same things in the same ways, the results will always be the same. That reluctance to change won't move us forward.

Safety Issues

Church communities are increasingly becoming aware of the importance of individual and collective safety. Churches that have had the misfortune of an accident or impropriety and subsequent lawsuits have suffered greatly. Youth and adult leaders who have been involved in such situations feel pain as well. Dealing with potential problems before they occur will prevent much heartache.

Insurance

Is your local church's insurance adequate to cover the group when they go off of the church property? Do you need additional insurance for higher risk activities such as snow sports, ropes course, water sports, rock climbing and rappelling? Check with your church office to determine who has the answers to these questions.

Once you have obtained the information, share it with the parents so that they understand how the insurance coverage works in your situation. In most cases, the insurance of the individual teen or family provides the primary coverage and the church insurance provides the secondary insurance. The medical form (see sample on page 99), which parents or guardians sign, reinforces their responsibilities by stating they will be accountable for all medical expenses incurred in an emergency. If your church's insurance coverage differs from this description, explain your particular coverage to the parents.

Some insurance carriers require specific guidelines and policies related to health and safety issues both for youth and for adults who work with teens. They may require all adults in contact with youth on a regular basis to fill out volunteer disclosure forms. Some also require you to keep medical authorization forms current in case of injuries and to set and enforce policies about transportation. Even if insurance has minimal requirements, you may want to go the full route. Good policies and procedures can prevent many bad situations.

Transportation Policy

All persons driving youth during a group activity should be at least twenty-one years of age, have a current driver's license, and be driving well-maintained vehicles. No youth should drive other teens during youth group

Policy Rules

It is tempting, especially in a single-digit youth group, to be casual about these kind of policies. However, the only way to assure safety is to always follow your policies, with no exceptions.

This strict adherence also takes the pressure off adults if youth try to convince them to make an exception. Adults can say they are not allowed to make that decision. The youth will stop asking for, or expecting, special permission.

activities and should only drive themselves if the destination is within a short distance of the church and their homes. Driving themselves during youth group activities should be a last resort and only with the permission from parents and the adult leaders. I highly recommend that your group adopt this policy.

It is tempting, especially in a single-digit youth group, to be casual about these kinds of policies. However, the only way to assure safety is to always follow your policies, with no exceptions.

This strict adherence also takes the pressure off adults if youth try to convince them to make an exception. Adults can say they are not allowed to make that decision. The youth will stop asking for, or expecting, special permission.

When you travel, always carry with you copies of signed medical release forms for each person. Should an accident happen, having information immediately available to emergency and hospital personnel could make a significant difference.

Safe Sanctuaries

Reducing the risk of abuse in youth ministries is important. Not everyone, even in a church, is exactly what he or she seems to be. Problems can arise, and although I hope you will never have an incident to deal with, you need to be taking preventative measures. Have procedures to minimize the risk of abuse and to guide you in responding to an incident. These procedures will also prepare you to deal with accusations of abuse, whether or not it actually has happened.

One of the best resources is *Safe Sanctuaries for Youth: Reducing the Risk of Abuse in Youth Ministries* by Joy Thornburg Melton. (For ordering information, see page 112.) This book includes background information, policies and procedures that assure better safety, and a process for developing your own church policy. Also included are a sample youth ministry staff worker position description and other sample forms.

If you don't already have a church youth ministry safety policy in place, here are several critical points I have gleaned from this book to get you thinking about areas to consider for your church's policy:

Screen All Adults

Churches should screen all of the adults who volunteer to work with children or youth in their congregations. According to Melton, "screening reduces the risk of a child abuser being recruited to work with your children, your church being accused of negligent hiring practices, [and] false allegations being brought against workers" (page 32). You can screen adults in various ways. With my youth group I provide a volunteer disclosure form to every adult who works directly with youth. The volunteers must fill out the form, sign it, date it, and return it to me. (See page 101 for sample form. *Safe Sanctuaries for Youth* also provides a volunteer application form on page 82.) A new form should be filled out each year so that the information is current. If someone does not want to fill out the form, give him or her the choice to either fill it out or be dropped from the volunteer list. If anyone indicates a history of any concern, evaluate whether or not that information indicates a future risk in the setting for which they are volunteering. Although such screening seems tedious, Melton argues that it is necessary:

> Abuse prevention and risk-reduction policies and procedures are essential for every congregation, not only for the protection and safety of our youth and children (all those under the age of eighteen) but also for our volunteer and paid workers with children and youth. Local congregations differ in the ways they engage in ministry with youth. Therefore, each congregation's need for prevention policies and guidelines will be somewhat different from the others.

> The gospel calls us to be engaged in ministry with youth. We must not allow the risks to undermine or stop our ministry. Rather, we must

> • acknowledge the risks and develop a practical plan to reduce them;
> • take steps to prevent harm to our youth and workers with youth;
> • continue to answer the gospel's imperative to be in ministry with youth, making a difference in their lives (page 8).[1]

The guidelines of one Protestant denomination describe more specifically what churches should do:

> God calls us to make our churches safe places, protecting children and other vulnerable persons from sexual and ritual abuse, God calls us to create communities of faith where children and adults grow safe and strong. In response to this churchwide challenge, the following steps should be taken to reduce the risk of child sexual abuse:

A. Local churches should

1. develop and implement an ongoing education plan for the congregation and its leaders on the reality of child abuse, risk factors leading to child abuse, and strategies for prevention;

2. adopt screening procedures (use of application forms, interviews, reference check, background clearance, and so forth) for workers (paid and unpaid) directly or indirectly involved in the care of children and youth;

3. develop and implement safety procedures for church activities such as having two or more non-related adults present in classroom or activity; leaving doors open and installing half-doors or windows in doors or halls; providing hall monitors; instituting sign-in and sign-out procedures for children ages ten or younger; and so forth;

4. advise children and young persons of an agency or a person outside as well as within the local church whom they can contact for advice and help if they have suffered abuse;

5. carry liability insurance that includes sexual abuse coverage;

6. assist the development of awareness and self-protection skills for children and youth through special curriculum and activities; and

7. be familiar with annual conference and other church policies regarding clergy sexual misconduct.[2]

Youth workers have not only a moral responsibility to youth but also a sacred responsibility. We are entrusted with the lives of young people so that they may grow closer to God, becoming faithful Christians. I see this obligation as an honor, so my behavior needs to show respect and honor God. If the youth trust the adults working with them, they will more often turn to those adults and their youth group peers about making decisions and addressing faith questions. Please consider what policies and procedures need to be in place to assure that the youth and adults who work with them are protected. Melton offers a few:

Appropriate Interpersonal Boundaries

Youth ministry can be described by many adjectives, but the first one is almost always relational. Youth get involved, and stay involved, with youth ministries because the ministries offer opportunities to experience relationships with peers and adults that are healthy, both physically and spiritually. Whether they can articulate this or not, the youth want and need to see good examples from the adult leaders of appropriate ways to relate to others. Adults who model respectful and nurturing behaviors that do not interfere with another's privacy provide these types of good examples. The youth will follow the lead of the adults in this regard; therefore, it is important for the adult workers to be clear about appropriate behaviors. Adult workers must be attentive to appropriate dress codes (some groups have found it effective to adopt actual dress codes for retreats, trips, and regular meetings), appropriate use of language, and appropriate demonstrations of affection and encouragement. A good rule of thumb for adults leaders is to never initiate a hug and to always be the one to end the hug. A retired junior high and high school educator put it this way, "If it's not yours, don't touch it." In other words, offer hugs when they are requested, but do not ever impose your touches on the youth in your group. whenever a question arises about where to draw appropriate interpersonal boundaries, remember than you are the adult and it is your responsibility to behave professionally, even if you are a volunteer.

The Two-Adult Rule

Simply stated, the two-adult rule requires no fewer than two adults present at all times during any church-sponsored program, event, or ministry involving youth. Risk will be reduced even more if the two adults are not related. The Sunday school class is always attended by at least two adults. A Bible study group for youth is always taught by at least two adults. The youth fellowship group is always staffed with at least two adult counselors/leaders.

The significance of this rule cannot be overstated. A church will drastically reduce the possibility of an incident of abuse if this rule is followed. Abusers thrive on secrecy, isolation, and their ability to manipulate their victims. When abusers know they will never have a chance to be alone with potential victims, they quickly lose interest in working with youth. Thus, the youth are protected, and the church has greatly reduced the likelihood of a claim that abuse has been perpetrated by one of its volunteers or workers and reduced the likelihood of a claim of negligence against the church. Furthermore, vigilant adherence to the two-adult rule provides important protection of the church's workers with children and youth. Even small churches can adhere to this rule by using assigned adult roamers, volunteers who move in and out of classrooms and recreation areas and function as additional helpers. Parents and youth who know that two adults will be present at all times are less likely to make false allegations, since it would be nearly impossible to prove allegations against two workers. Church members will be more confident when they volunteer to work with youth, because they will know that they will never bear the total burden of leadership and that the church has made a commitment to protecting them as well as the youth.[3]

Having two adults can feel overwhelming if you only have one youth, but there are ways to make even that situation safe. For a ministry involving one youth and one adult, consider meeting

- at a fast food restaurant where you can get a soft drink and hold discussion;
- outdoors for a service project;
- on the swing set at a school playground;
- outside the church on the lawn or bench;
- for a walk around the neighborhood for a discussion;
- at the home of the youth with a parent in the next room (with doors open);
- at your home with your spouse or other family member nearby (In homes never meet in a bedroom. Use the living room or kitchen.); at a picnic table in the park for a Bible study; or
- at a homeless shelter to serve a meal.

Always ask yourself how you can accomplish your particular program either in a public place or near another adult with open access. Maybe instead of holding a program in a closed room you could move it to a fellowship hall where anyone could enter at any time. Just do your best to make the youth group gatherings safe for both the adult and the teens. Encourage the one youth to invite a friend or two.

> ## Youth-to-Adult Ratios
>
> ### 1–3 Youth: 2 Adults
> (1 leader & 1 present, very nearby, or clearly visible)
>
> ### 4–6 Youth: 2 Adults
> (1 leader & 1 helper)
>
> ### 7–9 Youth: 2 Adults
> (1 leader & 1 participant/helper/leader)

The Five-Years-Older Rule

Often, especially in youth ministry, the people who volunteer to work with or who apply for a paid position are in college or have just graduated from college. If a junior in college (age twenty or twenty-one) is recruited as a counselor in the senior-high youth fellowship, the counselor may be leading youth who are only three or four years younger than he or she is. This should be prohibited for the protection of the youth and of the worker. Nearly every church has members who can remember a situation in which this rule was not followed and the people involved came to regret it. Do not make the same mistake. College students might be successful as workers with the junior-high youth, or the middle-high group; but they should not be given the sole responsibility for any group (page 39).

Open-Door Counseling

At any counseling sessions with youth, the door of the room used should remain open for the entire session. Ideally, the session will be conducted at a time when others are nearby, even if they are not within listening distance.[4]

Background Checks and Reporting Suspected Abuse

Some states allow you to request a criminal background and records check on volunteers or potential staff. In other states the police bureau cannot provide that information. You will need to check the statutes and services of your state to find out how to do a background check. You could hire private investigators, but they may charge hefty fees unless they belong to the church and are willing to offer discounts.

If you have reason to suspect that a youth in your group is the victim of abuse (physical, emotional, neglect, sexual, or ritual), you may be required to report. Check your state laws about reporting to find out what route to take. If you have questions, talk with the pastor or immediate supervisor about the proper procedures to secure help for your youth. Some things may be "beyond you," and it's wise to know when and where to request additional help so that you can handle possible abuse cases correctly.

Sleeping Arrangements and Time

Several times a year youth groups usually sleep overnight during a retreat, mission trip, or regional event. If the sleeping space provided is a common space such as the floor of a church or an outdoor field, designate one area for the girls that is separate from the guys' area. There should be some space in between—a good place for adults.

Nowadays youth groups commonly need to stay in hotel or dorm rooms when they travel rather than in larger common spaces. In those settings youth should stay with youth and adults with adults. No adults and youth should share rooms if at all possible. (Parents can be an exception.) If you have multiple youth rooms, have the adult rooms interspersed between youth rooms. You can more easily hear when they come and go or if they're up late and making noise. I also like to remind them about their responsibility to respect one another and the other hotel or dorm guests and to stay in their room at the agreed time. If they don't honor those requests, they may not have the same privileges the next time.

If you've arranged sleeping spaces for the group, require that the girls and guys stay out of the space belonging to the opposite sex, especially if they're staying in hotel rooms. If they want to gather as a group in one room for conversation or card games, they should get permission from the adult supervisors, keep the door open, and remain quiet enough to not bother others.

I also recommend having a policy on how many hours of sleep to allow during overnight trips with the youth group. Some events are intended to have activities in the middle of the night. However, if the retreat or event includes staying overnight for several days, consider allowing at least eight hours of sleep between lights-out time and wake-up time. Persons not needing as much sleep must remain quiet for those who need it.

We Did It This Way: Sleeping Arrangements

If room allows, another great way to separate girls from guys is to have all of the youth form a big circle and lie down with their heads pointing to the center and the adults at the transition points between boys and girls. This arrangement lets everyone feel part of the group, yet it automatically puts space between the sleeping bags. Remember, though, that at least one adult should be at each of the two transition points.

New research on the developing brain indicates that teenagers in general need a full night of sleep. You will find from experience that if they don't get adequate sleep, they tend to get grumpy or can't pay attention, symptoms that will affect the rest of the group. They may get a headache, fall asleep during group program time, or even catch a virus. We shouldn't have to send youth home sick because we didn't adequately provide for sleep. They shouldn't run ragged on the weekend and then be unable to attend or pay attention in school on Monday. When we become lenient about sleep time, we don't fulfill our responsibility as leaders.

When participating in a mission trip or week-long camp, allow for naps during the early afternoon. This time of rest can rejuvenate people, giving them more energy for the remainder of the day. Make sure that everyone remains quiet so that others can sleep.

Parents are entrusting us with the lives of their teens, so we must keep them safe and in a healthy environment. I don't want to talk with youth about taking care of their bodies and then do things that contradict what I've said.

> Parents are entrusting us with the lives of their teens, so we must keep them safe and in a healthy environment.

[1] Reprinted from *Safe Sanctuaries for Youth: Reducing the Risk of Abuse in Youth Ministries* by Joy Thornburg Melton. Copyright © 2003 Discipleship Resources. All rights reserved. Used by permission.

[2] Reprinted from *The Book of Resolutions of The United Methodist Church—2000*, page 181. Copyright © 2000 by The United Methodist Publishing House. Used by permission.

[3] *Safe Sanctuaries for Youth,* pp. 37–38.

[4] *Safe Sanctuaries for Youth,* p. 40.

7 42 Great Activities for Single-Digit Groups

Scripture Connections

Every week in youth group, I have the joy of teaching Scripture. Doing so is an important commitment, since the Bible teaches us how to live as disciples of Jesus Christ. By exposing youth to the Scriptures week after week, even if only briefly, we help them understand how the stories relate to their lives today. When they are faced with life's difficult choices, I hope that what they've learned in youth group will guide and comfort them.

> Youth: 1+
>
> Time: 5–15 minutes
>
> Supplies: Bibles
>
> Prep: Select and meditate on the chosen passage; study it

The youth need to have the Bible in their hands so that they can look up a passage each week and learn how to navigate through the Bible. I have had youth in my group who know the Bible inside out, as well as youth who don't know anything about the Bible. One day a teen came up to me after youth group and asked, "Why is there a book that's full of books? That's kinda weird!" These youth benefit from learning alongside peers, who, without judgment or ridicule, help them find a passage and patiently wait for everyone to find it before we start reading.

To use the Bible as a guide for their lives, teens need to get familiar with it, remember what they've read, look for particular stories or poems, ask questions, and struggle to understand the Scriptures' meaning. Youth cannot accomplish these tasks if they don't first have the Bible in their hands and become comfortable with it. So I try to always have a Scripture for everyone to look up, even if only one person reads it for the group. Sometimes they take turns reading longer passages. Having done so for months, they just expect the Bible reading and don't find it scary or weird. Here are some favorite passages to use:

Psalm 138 (God's steadfast love)
Micah 6:8 (What the Lord requires)
Matthew 5:13-16 (Light of the world)
Matthew 5:1-12 (The Beatitudes)
Matthew 7:7-12 (Ask, seek, knock)
Matthew 7:1-5 (Judge not)

Luke 11:33-36 (Light and darkness)
John 15:9-17 (Abide in my love)
Romans 8:24-33; 37-39 (Hope)
Hebrews 11:1 (Faith is . . .)
Philippians 2:13 (God is at work)
1 John 2:5-6, 10 (Walk as Jesus did)

Activities Index

Activities in this chapter are coded for the minimum number of youth needed, such as 2+, meaning two or more youth. These numbers are not the "recommended number" of participants for an activity; rather they tell you the activity works with that number or more. The numbers also assume that, in most cases, the adults present will also participate in the activity. If three or more youth are present, the adults may not need to do part of the activity. However, adults should participate in as much of the program as possible. If one adult gives directions, the second may get out supplies. But if the second adult is not needed for specific tasks, he or she should participate in the activity if able.

Some of the activities described here have a reproducible sheet, which you will find on the pages following the respective activity descriptions.

Additional activities that can easily accommodate a single-digit group are found in *Destination Unknown*, by Sam Halverson. (See page 112 for ordering information.)

We Did It This Way: Talking Tools

I have found that the youth pay more attention in our meeting time when I have a talking tool. It can be any item you have handy, but the more unusual it is, the better.

I started with a wand filled with floating stars. If someone wanted to talk, he or she had to have the wand, so only one person could talk at a time. When another person wanted to talk, that youth motioned that he or she wanted the wand. If a person was done talking, he or she offered the wand for whoever wanted to take it from there. Before too long, one youth brought a marble egg she found at a garage sale, so it became the talking egg. We have had talking potatoes, beach balls, flashlights, and so forth. Talking tools can be made up along the way and used as needed.

1 Preferences Icebreaker

Youth: 1+

Time: 5–20 minutes

Supplies: None

Prep: Make 1 copy of the questions for each person

Divide the youth into pairs. (If you have an uneven number of people, allow a group of three or have an adult pair up with a youth.) In pairs, the youth take turns asking each other the questions below, with both people answering each question. If you have multiple pairs, you may choose to have them switch partners anytime you say "switch."

You may use this entire list or just select your favorites, depending on how much time you have. If you want to add to this activity, ask the youth to tell their partners one new thing they've learned about them or what surprised them most about their partners' answers.

Would you prefer to . . .

- read a book or listen to music?

- eat thick-crust pizza or thin-crust pizza?

- have no values or no friends?

- be lost in a jungle or in a desert?

- go swimming or hiking?

- be an only child or one of ten children?

- drink diet or regular soft drinks?

- admit to a fear or do something you were afraid of doing?

- watch a sunset or a sunrise?

- go deaf or go blind?

- browse a book store or a music store?

- be gossiped about or lied to?

- play a sport or be a spectator?

- have a great sense of humor or have fame?

- read the book first or see the movie first?

- be afraid of the dark or be claustrophobic?

- eat squid or chocolate covered ants?

- swim like a fish or fly like a bird?

- have a whole lot of OK friends or one really great friend?

- be admired for what you say or for what you do?

- work in a crowd of people or work alone?

- ride in a horse-drawn carriage or a race car?

- take a picture of someone or have someone take a picture of you?

- be the teacher or the student?

- play a piccolo or a tuba?

2 Journal Making

In this activity, each youth makes a journal to keep and use. You may do as much or as little preparation of the materials as you feel is appropriate for your particular group. Be sure each person puts his or her name on the outside, so that others don't have to open it to know to whom it belongs.

Begin the journal writing by having the group write in response to something you read or show them. Use your imagination when providing topics to write about. If you can, store the journals safely in your regular meeting space so that the youth may write in them during other meeting times. Have the youth take their journals on mission trips, retreats, and other events that offer time for reflection.

At a graduation celebration give the youth their journals to keep. Write a special letter of your own about the youth to include also.

Youth: 1+

Time: 30–60 minutes

Prep: Gather supplies, cut the material for the cover to 8-1/2" x 5-1/2" and cut the sheets of paper in half. Set out materials.

Supplies: 100 8-1/2" x 11" sheets of paper per person; cardstock or other material for cover; hole punch; rings or other materials to hold booklet together; rulers; pens, markers, paper, glue, and anything else to decorate cover

3 Devotional

Invite the youth to read a devotional to the group. You or the youth can read the group through the accompanying questions, or invite discussion by asking questions such as: Where do you connect with the story?

One of the best youth devotional magazines available is *Devo'Zine*. (For ordering information, see page 112.) You may wish to subscribe to the magazine for all of your youth to help them begin holy habits of devotional reading on their own, as well.

You can easily include devotionals in your group meetings. You may want to use them each time you meet.

Youth: 1+

Time: 10 minutes

Supplies: Devotional book or magazine

Prep: Either select or have a youth select the devotional to read

4 Collecting for Those in Need

Announce what you are collecting (food, blankets, socks), who it is for, and the deadline for bringing it to the church. Decide whether you want to offer pickup service or not. Once the items are collected, go as a group to deliver them if you can.

Youth: 1+

Time: 1–2 hours

Supplies: Boxes and/or bags for collection sites at the church

Prep: Determine what agency will receive the collected items and select the delivery date. Put an announcement in worship bulletin, church newsletter, or on a poster.

5 Where Will You Go From Here?

Distribute the questions sheets and say: "At the beginning of a new year we have an opportunity to reflect on our lives and how we can move forward. Although this reflection is introspective, we can learn a lot about ourselves by discussing our lives with the youth group. We don't have to wait until New Year's to do this process; we can do so any day of our lives. But the beginning of a new calendar year will more likely remind us to use this time mark to turn our lives in a new direction. Maybe we want to learn a new skill or change some aspect of ourselves.

"I have given you a set of questions to think about and respond to. Find a quiet space away from everyone else, read through the questions, and take time to think about your life. Then fill in your answers. After fifteen minutes, we will come back together, and you can choose which answers you are willing to discuss with the group."

Where Will You Go From Here?

What do you want to stop in your life?

What is something you really want to go for in the coming year?

What is something you want to work on?

What is something you need to let go of in the coming year?

Who is someone you need to forgive?

Who is someone you would like to get to know better in the coming year?

What is something you have procrastinated about and need to do now?

What would you like God to help you with?

6 Did You Know?

Youth: 1+

Time: 15–30 minutes

Supplies: Handouts and pens or pencils

Prep: Make copies of the handout below

Complete the sentences; then we will talk about the ones you choose to discuss.

I am at my best when...

What I like best about school is...

The best thing that could happen to me would be...

I wish my friends or my family knew...

I REALLY ENJOY...

When I am proud of myself I...

I wish my parents knew that...

when i don't like something i've done, i...

I WOULD LIKE TO...

One of my favorite things to do in my free time is...

Three things I would like this youth group to be are...

7 Give It Up, Will You?

Youth: 1+

Time: 15 minutes

Supplies: none

Prep: none

Read aloud Mark 6:7-13 (Sending out the Twelve). Then talk about these questions:

• Have you ever been asked to give up a possession?

• If Jesus were to arrive here now and ask you to leave everything behind except two things, what two possessions would you take with you? Why?

• If you were one of the twelve disciples and left all but two things behind, how would you use what you took with you to serve God?

8 "You Choose" Bible Study

Youth: 1+

Time: 30 minutes

Prep: None

Supplies: Bible, pen and paper for each person

For this type of Bible study, select a Bible passage of interest. Try the format below for exploring the passage.

Read the Scripture aloud, using several different translations if you have them.

Now discuss the context of what comes before and after the passage read. Ask the youth who might be writing or speaking and what the passage was originally about.

Next, select key words or short phrases from the Scripture, and try to think of synonyms or paraphrases for those words or phrases.

• Do the meanings of the Scripture's words today differ from what their meanings were when they were written? If so, what's different?

• If this passage were written today, how might you paraphrase it in everyday language?

• What does this passage say about how you live your life?

• Do you agree with what it's saying?

• If you were to apply this Scripture, would you need to change anything in order to apply this to your life?

9 Pick-It-Up Service Project

This project is a great activity to do with one or more youth. Since you will be outside, it's also an acceptable one to do if only one adult is available to lead the group. If you have the supplies on hand, it's also a good one to do on the spur of the moment in case you need to change plans for some reason.

This project has a simple goal: to clean up the church's neighborhood. If the area is safe enough, you can support your immediate neighborhood without being intrusive. Work in a small group of two or three or in multiple small groups on opposite sides of the street. Walk on the sidewalk, if one is available, and collect trash that has accumulated on the ground along the sidewalk or parking strip. Determine whether or not it is safe to include the gutter area along the curb, if there is one. Youth should not walk in the street. Make sure the teens wear gloves and use tongs or grippers when picking up items such as broken glass. Depending on the neighborhood, there may even be riskier items such as hypodermic needles or condoms. Tell the youth to not pick up needles unless the cap is on and they can do it with tongs or grippers. Tell them to never pick up anything that appears to have blood on it.

During the pick-it-up walk, you may choose to talk about keeping your environment clean and safe. Or you may want to just visit and enjoy the walk. Either way, you are doing a service to your neighborhood (or whatever area you choose to clean up).

When you return, throw out your garbage bags in the church's garbage pickup container or dumpster. Also throw away latex gloves. If you use rubber gloves of higher value, turn them inside out as you take them off and wash them in hot, soapy water when you get inside.

Youth: 1+

Time: 15 minutes to as many hours as you choose

Supplies: A large, thick garbage bag and latex or rubber gloves for each person; tongs or long gripping devises if available (can be shared)

Prep: Notify the youth to wear closed-toed shoes and be prepared to do some walking; gather supplies; determine route; have transportation available if needed.

10 Newsroom Tour

Be sure to take a list of questions to the news station. A common one is "How do you decide what to report?"

After the tour, talk about what the youth found interesting and what they learned. Ask whether they will view the news reports differently now that they've toured behind the scenes.

Youth: 1+

Time: 1 hour probably

Supplies: List of questions

Prep: Find a news station that will provide a tour for your group and answer questions about news reporting. Perhaps one of your relatives or someone in your church works at a station. If not, just ask. If you need to travel to another town to get to a news station, arrange transportation and get parental permission. Prepare a list of questions the youth would like to ask.

11 Card Making for Those in Need

Card-making gives youth a chance to be creative and make people feel good at the same time. Service agencies usually want cards decorated on the front and saying, "Happy Birthday" or "Merry Christmas." The inside can be blank so that the agency's employees can write their own notes to their clients. Just ask what they would like.

Youth: 1+

Time: 1-1/2 to 3 hours

Supplies: Construction paper or pre-scored greeting cards; matching-size envelopes; double-stick tape, glue sticks, or craft glue; scissors for each person; decorative papers (such as wrapping paper); other flat items to add interest to the card, such as stickers; colored pens or fine-point markers; stencils or rubber stamps (optional)

Prep: Determine what agency or group of people you are making the cards for, gather supplies, and prepare work table(s).

12 Service Project: Soup Kitchen

Volunteer to serve a meal at a soup kitchen or other service bureau for homeless and hungry people. To prepare, discuss the following questions with the youth:

- What are some unpleasant things you might see?

- What are some neat things you might experience?

- What are some of the feelings you might have while there?

- What do you hope to learn?

Youth: 1+

Time: 1 hour or more

Supplies: None

Prep: Contact an agency for which you can volunteer; schedule a date and time

Talk over safety issues (such as not giving out your full name and staying with the group or assigned area). Don't be afraid of the people you are serving. The environment in which you will serve already takes precautions and has things set up in a way that works best. Don't forget to smile and say hello to the people coming through the line. As you serve, think of things you'd like to discuss with the group after finishing your work. Be sure to have that debriefing conversation.

13 The Lord's Prayer: Then and Now

Distribute the duplicated sheets and say: "Most people who have attended church regularly have memorized the Lord's Prayer, because they have repeated it during worship. But how often do we ponder each phrase and its full meaning? The most familiar version of the prayer is based on Matthew 6:8-13. You can read it in several translations.

"Our task is to create a paraphrase of the Lord's Prayer, rewriting each phrase in our own words. The phrases are listed below on the left side of the page. Think about what each phrase means and brainstorm ways to say the phrase in other words. Then write the new phrase on the right side of the page, across from the original one. This activity will give us new thoughts about the meaning of the prayer to reflect on each time we hear or say it in worship or during our own prayer time."

Youth: 1+

Time: One hour

Supplies: Bible, handout, and pen for each person; scissors

Prep: Duplicate the handout below; cut at the dotted line.

- -

Our Father,	_____

who art in heaven,	_____

hallowed be thy name.	_____

Thy kingdom come.	_____

Thy will be done on earth	_____

as it is in heaven.	_____

Give us this day our daily bread	_____

and forgive us our trespasses (or debts)	_____

as we forgive those who trespass against us.	_____

And lead us not into temptation	_____

but deliver us from evil;	_____

for thine is the kingdom	_____

and the power	_____

and the glory	_____

forever.	_____

Amen.	_____

- -

14 Collage: It's All About Me!

Youth: 1+

Time: 45–60 minutes

Supplies: Any printed material that can be cut up, such as magazines; scissors for each person; glue sticks, one piece of large, heavy paper per person; thin markers

Prep: Gather supplies, cover the work space with paper or plastic.

Youth and adults alike will enjoy this project. As you might have guessed by the title, individuals will be creating a collage that expresses who they are, what they like or enjoy, and their thoughts and opinions. Tell the youth that they may use their creativity to overlap cutouts, add words, or make borders. The only restriction is to keep the collage appropriate for youth group, avoiding inappropriate words or photos.

When the youth are finished, give each person an opportunity to tell the others about his or her collage, so that everyone may learn something new about the teen. Display the collages on a wall or door and either leave them up for a while or save them to make a group collage later. If you would like temporary wall space, use rolling dividers on which you can post the group's work. When other groups use the room, you can store the divider against the wall with the youths' work hidden.

15 Service Project in Your Church

Youth: 1+

Time: Depends on project

Supplies: Depends on project

Prep: Talk with the pastor or other church staff about the work that needs to be done and pick a project. Schedule a time to do the work.

We usually think about going somewhere else to do service projects, forgetting that our churches often need volunteers to do work on the building or yard. Try to match the skills and interests of the youth with the jobs that need to be done. You may suggest jobs they hadn't thought of.

One of my favorite church service projects is to wash the toys in the nursery so that the children will have clean toys to chew on. Other ideas include

• having a toy drive for low-income children or a shelter

• deep-cleaning the pews or chairs in the sanctuary

• deep-cleaning the kitchen

• painting

• moving furniture

• taking out the recycling if it doesn't get picked up by a service

• pulling weeds or planting flowers in the flower beds

16 Prayer Planting

This activity is simple but can be very important. As the youth put each plant in the ground, they say a prayer for a youth whom they know and who needs prayers or friends. They should think of people that no one else may be praying for or caring about. Through this act of intercessory prayer, lives can be changed.

After the planting is done, close with a time of reflection about the experience and a prayer for God to continue to use the youth group.

Youth: 1+

Time: 2 hours

Supplies: Bedding plants, bag of soil, bucket for water, gloves, small shovel, and hand tools of your choosing

Prep: Get permission to plant bedding plants at the church or at a church member's home where he or she is unable to do yard work. Schedule work time.

17 All That Sanctuary Stuff

Take a tour of the sanctuary of your church and ask the pastor to explain the symbolism, purpose, and meaning of the names of the various worship items such as the eternal flame, pulpit, and so forth. Look carefully at the stained glass windows too. See if he or she tells you something you don't already know.

Youth: 1+

Time: 20-30 minutes

Supplies: None

Prep: Ask the pastor to join you for this tour.

18 Help Out Your Pastor

For this project you and the youth will meet with the pastor to get information on the Scripture and the points of the sermon that he or she is planning. Work together to list the ideas and phrases you would like to include. Then rearrange the ideas in an order that can be read as liturgy, changing any words that don't flow well when read aloud. Complete it and turn it in to the pastor for inclusion in the worship bulletin. One or more of the youth may also help lead worship on the Sunday the liturgy is used.

Youth: 1+

Time: 2 hours

Supplies: Pen, sheet of paper, and Bible for each person

Prep: Get permission from the pastor to help with a Sunday worship service by writing liturgy to go with the Scripture and sermon selected.

19 Building a Group Covenant

Use this guide to discuss what elements to include in a group covenant. Focusing on certain issues, such as the ones below, will give you a more specific group covenant. See the sample covenant on the next page to get an idea of what kinds of answers the youth may come to. The final covenant should describe what the group is about and who you want to be when you're together.

Youth: 2+

Supplies: plain sheet of paper or large sheet of paper; marker

Prep: Gather supplies.

Step 1: As a group, read these covenant-building Scriptures:

Matthew 25:34-40; Luke 9:48; Romans 12:9-18; 1 Corinthians 12:12, 13:4-7; Galatians 5:22-26; 6:1-10; Colossians 4:5-6.

Step 2: Ask your group these questions and make a list of the answers:

When this group is together . . .

• What values or qualities are important to you (for example, honesty, integrity, kindness, a positive outlook, learning, sharing)?

• What do you want or need from the group (for example, respect, acceptance, caring, no put-downs or name-calling)?

• What are you willing to give to the group (for example, consistent attendance, participation, leadership)?

• What are the feelings you hope to have about the group (for example, belonging, community, fun)?

• What keeps you from having these feelings (for example, words, actions, fears, past experiences)?

• What should the group be able to expect from the leaders (for example, be on time, begin on time, no put-downs or name calling, limit inside jokes, acceptance, knowledge, compassion, safety, confidentiality within safety limits)?

Step 3: Have the group work with the list just created.

Make the individual words or groupings into short phrases (see the sample covenant). Then ask:

• Which of these items are you all willing to agree on and live up to?

• Are there any items you aren't willing to adopt?

• What will help you keep this covenant?

If you have a large piece of paper, transfer each of the phrases onto the sheet and leave it on the wall of your meeting space. Otherwise, write the list on a plain sheet of paper and ask all of the group members to sign it. Use the covenant as a tool to live by and reference if problems arise later.

SAMPLE GROUP COVENANT

We will do our best to help make our youth group a place of Christian community by living with these expectations:

- We agree to participate and make every effort to function as a team and care for one another.

- We will stay focused on God and our relationships with God.

- We will be sensitive to one another's needs and try to include everyone so that they feel accepted and important to the group.

- We will treat one another with respect and remember when it's time to play and when it's time to be more serious.

- We will listen to one another, especially when others are talking in group discussions, and try to hear what's being said.

- We will help to make our group a safe place by avoiding name-calling, insensitive teasing, and inappropriate sarcasm and put-downs.

- We will keep personal conversations confidential (as long as no safety or legal issue is involved).

- We will be honest, trustworthy, and supportive for our group.

- We will be on time to gatherings and make every effort to attend every session so that others can count on us.

- We will pray for one another as caring and loving Christians.

20 Take a Hike

While hiking, pay special attention to the many species of plants, trees, insects, and other creatures God has made. Give thanks to God for the beauty that surrounds you and the amazing cycle of nature that brings us food, clean air, renewal, and wonder. Along the way, invite the youth to relay to the group what they discover. Pick up the litter that has been left by previous visitors and put it in the trash bag.

Youth: 2+

Time: 2–4 hours

Supplies: A pair of walking shoes and a water bottle for each person; food if the trip lasts more than 2 hours; map; cell phone, radio, or other safety contact device; Bible; trash bag

Prep: Research good hiking areas and select a place to go. Arrange transportation.

21 Come to the Water

Gather and travel to the waterside spot selected. Find a comfortable spot to sit together. Then take turns reading the following Scriptures aloud:

- Psalm 1:1-3 (Tree planted by streams of water)
- Matthew 3:13-17 (Jesus baptized by John)
- Matthew 28:16-20 (The Great Commission)
- Mark 1:1-8 (John the Baptist)
- Mark 1:9-12 (Calling of the first disciples)
- Mark 1:14-19 (Calling of the first disciples)
- Luke 3:21-22 (Baptism of Jesus)
- John 2:1-11 (Jesus changes water into wine)
- John 4:1-26 (Samaritan woman at the well)
- Romans 6:3-11 (Dead to sin, alive in Christ)
- Titus 3:1-8 (Doing what is good; saved by the washing of rebirth)

Reflection Questions

Now discuss the following questions:

➡ What does the symbol of water tell us?

➡ Why does water matter in our lives?

➡ Is the role of water in baptism anything like the role of water in Holy Communion?

➡ In what ways do we use water in our daily lives?

➡ How, do you think, did the fishermen feel when Jesus asked them to leave their livelihood and follow him?

➡ Can we live without water?

➡ Can we truly live the life Christ intends for us without his water?

➡ Jesus still calls us today. What do you need to leave behind in order to follow him?

Ask the group to come close to the water's edge, if possible. Otherwise, dip a cup of water from the source. Say, "Dip into the water of earth and remember the water of life." Invite the youth to dip their hands or fingers into the water.

While their hands are still wet, offer this prayer: "God, we come to the water today to be refreshed and renewed by your love. Quench our thirst and make us clean so we can be faithful disciples of Jesus Christ in all that we do and say. Purify our hearts and minds, and make us whole. Amen."

Youth: 2+

Time: 1-1/2 hours, plus travel time

Supplies: Bibles, cup for water if the group won't be able to reach the body of water with their own hands

Prep: Find an appropriate place nearby where the youth group can meet at the waterside (lake, river, creek, pond) and can touch the water. Arrange transportation, planning for at least one vehicle to take group to the waterside.

22 Decorate Their World

Many nursing homes and other such agencies decorate for the various seasons and holidays, but not every place can afford to do any of these extras. Having colorful decorations in their living rooms or on their individual doors can really brighten people's lives. Ask the agency what kind of decorations it would like. If you can, take a brief tour in advance in order to take some measurements of specific windows, doors, and so on to you'll know what you have to work with and whether you can use tape and other supplies.

Have one or two sessions with the youth group just for making the decorations so that they are ready to put up. Then the day of the activity you can take the decorations to the site, meet some of the residents, put up decorations, and do some visiting or singing. Adapt what you do to the interests and skills of your group. There's no right or wrong way to do this activity. Your care will be appreciated.

Youth: 2+

Time: 2 hours

Supplies: Depends on project

Prep: One advance session with the youth to make the decorations; arrangements with a local nursing home, adult care center, residence hotel, or other selected agency

23 Conversation Cards

Conversation cards are great to have on hand when you are traveling, end an activity sooner than planned, or need to make a sudden change in a program. Once made, they will be ready to use anytime you want.

These cards have two questions labeled A and B. The person who is answering chooses A or B without seeing the questions. The youth can be asked these questions in a variety of ways:

1. Have each person take turns drawing a card and answering the questions it asks them. They may choose whether to answer Question A or B.

2. Ask the youth to form a circle, and then hand out the cards to everyone at once. Have one player ask the person to his or her left which question he or she wants to answer. Then have that person answer the question chosen. Then have the person who is answering ask the person to his or her left, and so on. Continue around the circle, or go back and forth if there are two or three people. You can shuffle and go through the cards as many times as you want.

3. Play a board game using the conversation cards instead of the board game's cards. Be sure to sort through the cards in advance and remove any you do not want to use.

4. Your youth may enjoy making up questions for a set of cards.

Youth: 2+

Time: 15–45 minutes

Supplies: Paper

Prep: Make the conversation cards by duplicating the card sheets on pages 68–69 and cutting the cards apart.

(You can add as many cards as you like by using a word-processing application to type them and cutting them apart.)

CONVERSATION CARDS

Ask your partner to choose A or B.

A. If your friends were to describe your family, what might they say?

B. What is your favorite childhood memory?

CONVERSATION CARDS

Ask your partner to choose A or B.

A. What do you tend to daydream about?

B. What's your biggest fear?

CONVERSATION CARDS

Ask your partner to choose A or B.

A. Who is someone you admire, and why?

B. What is the best thing about your church?

CONVERSATION CARDS

Ask your partner to choose A or B.

A. If you wanted to go to a peaceful place, where would you go?

B. What kind of work would you like to do in the future?

CONVERSATION CARDS

Ask your partner to choose A or B.

A. When are you the happiest?

B. What is one job you would never want to have to do?

CONVERSATION CARDS

Ask your partner to choose A or B.

A. What's the best thing about school?

B. How many years would you like to live?

CONVERSATION CARDS

Ask your partner to choose A or B.

A. What's something you can do that most people don't know about?

B. What would be your favorite place to have a picnic?

CONVERSATION CARDS

Ask your partner to choose A or B.

A. What is one skill you wish you had?

B. What trait do you hope you inherited from your parents?

CONVERSATION CARDS

Ask your partner to choose A or B.

A. Where would you like to be living ten years from now?

B. What's your favorite Christmas tradition?

CONVERSATION CARDS

Ask your partner to choose A or B.

A. What do you most admire about a good friend of yours?

B. What makes you feel valued?

CONVERSATION CARDS

Ask your partner to choose A or B.

A. What's the most foolish thing you've ever done?

B. Who is your favorite action hero?

CONVERSATION CARDS

Ask your partner to choose A or B.

A. How well do you think your parents listen to you?

B. What is something you'd like to know about the opposite sex?

CONVERSATION CARDS

Ask your partner to choose A or B.

A. What is your greatest accomplishment?

B. What are two important qualities of a friendship?

CONVERSATION CARDS

Ask your partner to choose A or B.

A. If you could ask God for only one thing, what would it be?

B. Would you prefer to be a leader or a follower?

CONVERSATION CARDS

Ask your partner to choose A or B.

A. If you met Jesus at the mall, what would you ask him?

B. What do you think is your best quality?

CONVERSATION CARDS

Ask your partner to choose A or B.

A. What is something you would like to do less of?

B. What or who has most influenced your faith?

CONVERSATION CARDS

Ask your partner to choose A or B.

A. What is one thing that hurts you?

B. What is the best thing about your best friend?

CONVERSATION CARDS

Ask your partner to choose A or B.

A. If you could have any pet, what would it be?

B. Who or what has been the most helpful in your life?

CONVERSATION CARDS

Ask your partner to choose A or B.

A. Who is someone you would like to meet?

B. What job would be your favorite if money weren't a concern?

CONVERSATION CARDS

Ask your partner to choose A or B.

A. When was the last time you talked to God?

B. Do you ever wish you had a sibling or another sibling?

CONVERSATION CARDS

Ask your partner to choose A or B.

A. If you were given a million dollars, what would you do with it?

B. What is something you like about our youth group?

CONVERSATION CARDS

Ask your partner to choose A or B.

A. What do you think is the hardest thing about being a parent?

B. If you could visit any country, which one would you visit?

CONVERSATION CARDS

Ask your partner to choose A or B.

A. What part of your life is the best?

B. When do you enjoy time alone?

CONVERSATION CARDS

Ask your partner to choose A or B.

A. Would you prefer to ride a Ferris wheel or a roller coaster?

B. How many states in the US have you been in?

CONVERSATION CARDS

Ask your partner to choose A or B.

A. What is something that makes you angry?

B. What are you willing to live for?

CONVERSATION CARDS

Ask your partner to choose A or B.

A. Do you dream in color or in black and white?

B. What's your favorite website?

CONVERSATION CARDS

Ask your partner to choose A or B.

A. What will you do when a friend hands you an alcoholic drink?

B. What is your favorite milk shake?

CONVERSATION CARDS

Ask your partner to choose A or B.

A. What is something that disappoints you?

B. What are five things you are thankful for?

CONVERSATION CARDS

Ask your partner to choose A or B.

A. What is a habit you would like to give up?

B. How much time do you spend on the phone each week?

CONVERSATION CARDS

Ask your partner to choose A or B.

A. What is something you would be willing to die for?

B. What is a talent or skill you hope to attain?

CONVERSATION CARDS

Ask your partner to choose A or B.

A. How can others tell when you're unhappy?

B. What is the most boring task you can think of?

CONVERSATION CARDS

Ask your partner to choose A or B.

A. When was the last time you stayed up all night?

B. What was the best gift you ever gave someone?

24 Background Check

Youth: 2+

Time: 45 minutes

Supplies: chair for each person, table, protective table cover such as newsprint or plastic, watercolors (1 for every 2 people), brushes, watercolor paper (1-1/2 sheets per person), scissors (optional) paper towels, masking tape, one paper or plastic cup per person, 2 pitchers or buckets. (One pitcher will serve to pour clean water into cups, and the youth can pour dirty water into the other to refresh their water while painting.)

Prep: Gather supplies; if necessary, cut one sheet in half for every two youth; put protective cover over the table, fill one pitcher with water, and put supplies on table.

Say: "Today we're going to do a background check on each of you. But instead of someone else looking into your past, you get to paint your background onto your watercolor paper. Before we begin painting, I am going to ask you some questions to think about followed by three minutes of complete silence. Here are the questions:

- What has your life been like in the past?

- Have you done things you now know are wrong?

- Have you been honest, caring, kind, and helpful to others?

- Have you been good to yourself (your body and your spirit)?

- Do you have secrets you don't want discovered?

- Do you have bad habits that need to change?

- Does your past bring you any sadness? joy?

- Have you been a good steward of the environment?

- Is there anything you are ashamed of?

Time three minutes of silence. Then say: "With the watercolors, I want you to paint your background based on what you've just been thinking about. Dark colors can represent sadness, shame, guilt, loneliness, bad habits, secrets, how you've poorly treated others or yourself, and so forth. The light or bright colors can represent joy, accomplishments, peace, health, positive attitude, problems resolved, relationships healed, and so forth. Your paper needs to be completely covered with only color, not specific items, like the background for a painting. If some periods of time in your past were better or worse than others, your background might change colors across the page. The great thing about this kind of background check is that only you and God know what your colors represent. I'll invite you but not require you to discuss something about your painting. Pour water into your cup until it's about two-thirds full. As it gets dirty, you can pour it into the other pitcher and refill your cup with clean water. Use a large sheet of watercolor paper. You have ten minutes."

After nine minutes ask the youth to finish within one minute. Then call time and ask them to rinse their brushes and wait for instructions. When the teens are ready, invite them to either describe their paintings or briefly discuss what they experienced while painting or thinking about the questions. Remind them they are not required to reveal anything they don't want to disclose.

After the teens have discussed, say: "Now that you've painted your background, you have an opportunity to put your future on top of it. Regardless of what you've done in the past, you can choose much of what

70

your future looks like. Using a small sheet of watercolor paper, paint your future. You can't know what things might happen to change your expectations, but paint the future you want to have. Here are some questions that might help guide your painting:

• What will you choose to do differently?

• Will you treat others or yourself better?

• Will you make an effort to be more honest and caring?

• How would you like others to see you?

• Will you make better choices?

• How bright will your future be?

Tell the youth they have ten minutes. After nine minutes, announce one minute to finish. Then call time. Ask the following questions, inviting responses:

• How was painting your future different from painting your past?

• Did you feel optimistic while painting?

• Have you made any resolutions to yourself about making changes?

• Are there things you are determined to do differently?

• How does it feel to have a fresh start?

When discussion is finished, have the teens blot their backgrounds with paper towels if the paintings have not dried yet. Then ask the youth to put their future paintings on top of their background paintings. The background should show around the edge like a frame. If the creations are dry enough, have the the youth tape their future paintings to their background paintings and leave them to dry.

Close with this prayer:

"God of darkness and light, we ask your forgiveness for things we have done in our past that did not honor you, our friends and family, ourselves, or your creation. We thank you for the chance to paint a brighter future and ask that you guide our watercolors of life. Shape our future selves into what you desire us to be. Help us to make good choices and wise decisions, so that we honor you in all that we do. Amen."

25 Farm-Crop Gleaning

Youth: 2+

Time: 1 day or more

Supplies: Gloves; other supplies depend on project.

Prep: Locate a farm that will donate crops for you to glean, so that you may give the produce to a food bank or meal-service agency.

If you live in an area with nearby farms, negotiate with their owners so that your group may do crop gleaning. Or you may have an agency that processes gleaned foods and could use your help. Check for options in your area.

Talk about the biblical connections to this activity. The youth may recall the story of Ruth. Have them also read Deuteronomy 24:19-22. Gleaning was an established practice, but anyone could gather what was left in the fields. God put a new focus on an old practice. This commandment to leave a bit behind in the fields after harvest comes from God's concern for the people on the margins of society. In the culture of that time the "alien, orphan, and widow" were groups of people who did not have family to provide for them and consequently were often destitute. Verse 22 is God's reminder to Israel that except for God's grace they themselves would be on the margins of Egyptian society.

Ask:

• Who in our society are the people shoved to the margins?

• How have you experienced God's grace?

• How can what we do be an instrument of God's grace?

26 Letters to God

Youth: 2+

Time: 30–45 minutes

Supplies: Pen for each person, journal or paper for each person

Prep: Gather supplies and duplicate the four letters on the following pages for each person.

Distribute the pens, handouts from pages 73–74, and journals or paper. Invite the youth to make a few notes of things in each letter that catch their attention. Ask for volunteers to read these four letters aloud for the group. When they are done reading, ask:

• Have you ever felt the same way or similar to the person in letter 1? 2? 3? 4?

• Do you agree or disagree with some of the statements or expressions in the letters?

Say: "Now write your own letter to God. Say whatever you want to say and thank God for hearing you." Allow the youth ten minutes to write.

Letter 1

Dear God,

I just wanted to stop by quickly and say hi. I feel like it's been forever since we last talked! How are you? I've been so busy lately that I just haven't had time to do much of anything, so that's probably why we haven't spent much time together lately, in case you were wondering. Sorry if you felt like I abandoned you or something, but really, I just haven't had any time!

But even though I've been so incredibly busy, the truth is I've missed you, God. I miss talking with you every day. I miss sharing the joys of my day with you, and I miss venting off my anger, frustrations, and sadness to you when I've had a bad day and nothing really seems to go right. My life just seems a little smoother when I spend some of it with you, God. When my life gets so crazy, I need you there with me to help me prioritize, organize, and calm my stress. We're like a team, you and I, so let's work together on this.

God, just help me see how important it is to spend time with you each day, help me to never think I'm too busy for you. To keep my faith in shape, I need to exercise daily. I need to walk with you.

Thanks for all your help and your listening ear. I can't wait to talk to you again soon!

Love,

Your friend

(written by Brittany Starr, at age 16)

Letter 2

Dear God,

Lately it seems like everyone has been talking about hope. "Put your hope in God," they say, or "God is your hope for better days." Well, I sure could use some better days ASAP! All these promises sound just great, but this "hope" business doesn't seem to be working very well.

I've prayed, put my trust in you, and decided to stop hoping and just let you do your magic. But, uh, God, I don't mean to be rude, but I think you may have forgotten about me. Since I've started letting you do your thing, nothing seems to have gotten better. I think things may have gotten worse!

So I've been searching for some sort of solution to this problem. Yesterday when I was talking to Mark, he gave me a few thoughts. He suggested that what I may need is some patience. I guess now that I think about that, it sort of makes sense. I mean, since you have led me this far, you probably have even better things in store for me, right? Mark also gave me this Scripture from Hebrews 11:1: "Now faith is being sure of what we hope for and certain of what we do not see" (NIV). I guess I do need to be certain of your plans for me. The last thing that Mark suggested to me is something I can make a daily habit of. He told me to make a list of five things you have done for me that I didn't expect. I'm going to put that list next to my bed, so that when I say my prayers at night, I'll remember that you may not answer my hopes and prayers exactly the way I want.

So I guess patience is a really important part of hope. If I hope for something, I have to put my patience in you to answer my prayers in your own way and time. So I'll try, God. I'll really try.

Love always,

Hopeful

(written by Beyth Hogue, at age 15)

Letter 3

Dear God,

Yesterday I was camping with my friend Megan. We had so much fun! We went hiking and swimming and got to sleep out under the stars! It seemed like I could feel your presence everywhere I went, but since Megan and her family aren't Christians, I couldn't really discuss these feelings with them.

It was so incredible how you seemed to be everywhere all at once! I wanted to sing the hymn "Pass It On." Like the song, I wanted to shout from the mountain top, to tell everyone that "the Lord of love has come to me." At the top of the mountain that Megan and I hiked, the sun was shining out from behind the trees in thick rays, reminding me how you reach out to every person individually, like those rays of sunshine.

As Megan and I were falling asleep, we began to talk about the stars. As it turned out, we had both been looking at the same one. You used this opportunity to remind me of how many people focus on the same thing I am and how I can use those people to help keep me on track.

Somehow, even after all of my cool God-sightings, I still couldn't bring myself to discuss my faith with Megan. Now that I'm back home, I'm going to have to put my faith in you to find a way to witness to Megan. She really needs that special and individual touch of yours, like the sunshine rays. I hope I can help keep her focused on the right thing. I know you are my hope. Now I just need a way to convince Megan of that.

Love,

Me

(written by Beyth Hogue, at age 15)

Letter 4

Dear God,

Hi there! How are you doing? I'm great! But I guess you already knew that, didn't you? In fact, you know everything there is to know about me! You probably know things about me that I don't even know yet! How do you do it, God? With the billions of people in the world, how do I fit in? How are you with me every second of every day when the six billion other people in the world need you just as much as I do? It's so amazing how you can be the best friend to everyone, how you can hear and answer all of our prayers at the same time. How can you listen to all of our prayers when we're all talking in different languages all at once? You somehow manage to make yourself known to each one of us and make us feel special and loved. You're so awesome, God, that it just blows my mind! I really don't know how you do it!

So I want to thank you so much, loving God, for holding me close to you and being my best friend. Thank you for also loving everyone else around me; it makes me feel closer to them just knowing that we share the same best friend. Thank you for blessing all of us with this family. With your help we can get through anything if we just stick together! Thanks so much, God, for being our strength and hope, and for showing us that we can have confidence in the future knowing that you'll be there beside us the whole way. Thank you for everything, God. I love you.

Love,

Your Child

(written by Brittany Starr, at age 16)

27 We Do Windows

This activity provides a fun way to help others by doing a task they find difficult or might otherwise have to pay someone to do. Get a list of people in your congregation, the church neighborhood, or wherever you want and call them to ask if your group could come and wash their outside windows for free.

Limiting the washing to the outside windows will keep you and the residents from worrying about tracking water or mud indoors. The limit will also keep you out of the residents' personal space, which they may not be comfortable with sharing. So pick a nice, warm day when cool water will be refreshing, and have fun while working!

Youth: 2+

Time: 1 hour or more (you decide)

Supplies: Addresses of place(s) where you are going to work; buckets; washing items such as brushes with handles, squeegees, hand mitts, liquid soap, mixable or spray glass cleaner, hose if one is not available at work site(s), towels for cleaning up and drying off

Prep: Get permission from people whose windows you want to wash and schedule the time with them. Ask them if they have a garden hose you can use. Gather supplies.

28 Rake and Run

In this activity the people you help may never know who helped them. There is something exciting about anonymously helping someone.

Gather addresses of church members (or other people you'd like to help) during autumn when the leaves are falling from the trees. Schedule an afternoon to go from home to home raking the leaves in their yards for free.

When you are done raking someone's yard, stick a calling card in his or her door. The cards, which can be typed or hand-written, may read:

We couldn't resist raking your leaves,
And we hope you won't think we are thieves.
We wanted to help, and we hope you won't yelp.
We are simply aiming to please!
        —The Rake & Run Team

Your group can do the same activity during other seasons and make up your own calling cards about shoveling snow, for example.

Youth: 2+

Time: 1–3 hours

Supplies: List of addresses, rakes, large leaf bags, Rake and Run calling cards

Prep: Decide where you want to visit, gather list of addresses, arrange transportation, and gather tools and supplies.

Youth: 2+

Time: 2 hours

Supplies: None

Prep: Locate the nearest ice skating or roller skating rink or a place to do a similar activity; determine the cost and tell the youth to bring that amount of money (plus snack money if appropriate); arrange transportation.

Youth: 2+

Time: 2–4 hours (depending on the length of the movie)

Prep: Several weeks ahead, have the youth group make a list of movies they would enjoy seeing and narrow it down. If the group cannot agree on one movie, take the top few and either choose for them or randomly select a movie. Obtain the movie for showing. Be sure you either meet in a home to watch the movie or have a video usage license for your church, so that you aren't breaking copyright laws. Otherwise, contact The Motion Picture Licensing Corporation's Church Desk 800-515-8855. Gather supplies. Invite the youth to bring a pillow and slippers for their comfort. Be sure to preview the movie before showing it.

Supplies: Video or DVD, VCR or DVD player, popcorn, and drinks

29 Just for Fun

Plan an afternoon or evening of fun going ice skating or roller skating. If those options aren't available, pick another recreational activity your group will enjoy. The purpose is to spend enjoyable time together, share a common experience, and have time for group building. This outing may also be a good time to ask your youth bring a friend or sibling. Use only your approved adult drivers and make sure a seat belt is available for every person.

30 Movie and Discussion

One of the best resources I have found for guiding movie discussion is *Reel to Real* (available on *ileadyouth.com*; see page 112). You can find others on the Internet or write your own.

Be sure to check the rating of the movie so that it fits the ages of your group members. Stick to this rule even if all of the youth tell you they have already seen a movie with a restricted (R) rating. The teens or their parents can choose for themselves, but when they attend a youth group function, you are responsible for adhering to guidelines.

31 Piece It Together: Mosaic

This hands-on exercise of creating a mosaic provides an opportunity for group building and creating something special.

Start with the framed backing lying on the table. Put the large piece of paper beside it. Explain to the youth the following options of how to design the layout:

• The group uses the plain paper to draw symbols it might want to create in tile. Then the group draws a master plan for the approximate look of the finished mosaic. You don't have to draw well, since the tiles won't be the size and shape of your drawing anyway. The drawing just gives you the basic idea of what you're going to create.

• The group lays out the tiles face up on the floor or plywood before sticking it to the backing. This method could spark ideas, such as using a certain color group to create a border or a center symbol, or you might disperse a color throughout the mosaic. You could include specific objects or symbols, or could make the mosaic more abstract. There's no right or wrong way to do this exercise—it can be as planned or as random as the group would like.

Once the group has chosen a plan and looked over the tiles, have one person apply a thick layer of adhesive to either the whole backing or to a section of it, depending on the size of the backing and how fast the adhesive will dry. Then begin setting the tiles. If the youth want to first set a border, symbol, or design, they can fill in the rest of the tiles around it. The colors of available tile pieces will determine how the mosaic turns out. So get creative and have fun!

Once the group has set the tiles, leave the mosaic to dry while cleaning up. At your next meeting, you can hang the picture or use it for a table top, altar piece, or anything else the group decides. The mosaic will be one of a kind, just like your group.

Youth: 2+

Time: 1–2 hours (or as long as you like)

Supplies: Plain paper, large piece of paper for the group to draw the plan on, pencil for each person, tiny or broken tiles for mosaic making, tile adhesive, mixing container (if needed), grout for mosaic, at least one trowel, adhesive applicators (tongue depressors or popsicle sticks work well), plywood board or other material appropriate for the backing, 2" x 2" framing strips for the plywood board

Prep: Gather supplies; make the backing board by cutting a piece of plywood any size you want to work with. (I recommend 20" x 30".) Nail the framing strips on top of the board at its edges to make a border. This border will "contain" your grout and tile. Find a table work space and cover it with plastic. Set out the supplies.

32 Is It Your Decision?

Youth: 2+

Time: 30–45 minutes

Supplies: one felt marker per person (different color per person if possible), extra sheets of paper for additional ideas, masking tape

Prep: Cut paper into 4-1/4" x 11" strips; write each of the decisions on a separate strip; tape each strip to a wall or door so that youth can walk up to it.

Write on the strips of paper:

What clothes you wear to school

How late you stay out at night

Going to church

How you spend your money

Cleaning your bedroom

Whether you get a tattoo

Trying out for athletic teams

Going to youth group

How you spend your summer

How you treat other people

Having a friend visit your home

When you start dating

Whether you give something away

Auditioning for the school play

Attending family events or activities

Doing something risky that might injure you

Choosing whom you hang out with

Playing the music you like

This activity aims to help youth identify what decisions they make for themselves and what decisions parents and other adults influence or determine. Some decisions, such as how they treat others, are their responsibility. Other decisions are privileges earned with age and experience; some may be prompted by God.

Invite the youth to come to the wall and mark the decisions on the strips of paper, using Y if the decision is their own or N if it's someone else's decision. Tell them to write a B next to a shared decision.

After the youth have marked all of the strips, invite the group to discuss any interesting discoveries they made. Then ask these questions:

• Are there any decisions you marked with an N that you feel you should be able to make at your age? If so, why, do you think, are you not allowed to make those decisions?

• Do your friends have the same freedoms or restrictions you have?

• Who are the people affected by the decisions you make?

• How does your faith influence what decisions you make?

• Do you find it sometimes hard to make decisions? If so, which ones are hardest?

• What could make them easier?

• Do you remember to pray about decisions you need to make?

Close with this prayer:

"God, you know our heads and hearts even better than we do. We ask your guidance in the decisions we are faced with. Give us a nudge in the best direction. Help us have the courage we need to make the right decisions— the ones you would want for us. Thank you for sending your Son, Jesus Christ, to show us the way. Amen."

33 How Can You Own the Wind?

Gather the youth in a comfortable space. Say: "Close your eyes and envision a lush, green forest with its creatures. . . . Picture a desert with sparse vegetation and the creatures that live there. . . . Now imagine a world where those places no longer exist." Invite them to open their eyes and listen to a story.

If you have *Brother Eagle, Sister Sky: A Message from Chief Seattle*, read the story to the youth, showing them the pictures. Also read the various Scriptures.

If you are unable to acquire *Brother Eagle, Sister Sky*, just read the Scriptures.

Ask the following questions for discussion:

• What does the earth give us?

• How do we use the earth?

• In what ways do we abuse the earth?

• Do you do things to help preserve the earth and the sky? If so, what do you do?

• What could we do differently that would help keep the earth healthy and vibrant?

When conversation has slowed, distribute a card and pencil to each person. Invite the youth to write a promise on their cards that they will fulfill to help keep the earth sacred.

If time allows, encourage the youth to discuss what they've written. Ask them to fold their cards in half, put them in a pocket, and take it home as a reminder of their promises and the goodness of the earth.

Youth: 2+

Time: 20–30 minutes

Supplies: Storybook *Brother Eagle, Sister Sky: A Message From Chief Seattle** (optional), index cards and pencils for each person, and a Bible

Prep: Gather supplies.

Objective: To reflect on the earth and all of its creatures as sacred; to help preserve our natural world.

Theme: Appreciating the earth and creation

Scripture:
Genesis 1:1-2, 4a
Romans 8:19-21
John 1:1-5, 14a
Psalm 24:1
Psalm 104:24-25
Romans 1:10-23

---

* *Brother Eagle, Sister Sky: A Message From Chief Seattle*. Illustrated by Susan Jeffers. New York: Dial Books, 1991.

Notes: There are several opinions about what Chief Seattle did and did not say. History seems to agree that Jeffers based the text of the book on the script Ted Perry wrote in 1971 for a movie called *Home*, produced by the Southern Baptist Convention Radio and Television Commission. Perry's script is a revision of a speech attributed to Chief Seattle, and he wrote the text as fiction for the movie, never intending it to be interpreted as the actual words of Chief Seattle. Regardless, this powerful and inspiring story is worthy of consideration.

Youth: 2+

Time: 1 hour

Supplies: Depends on project

Prep: Arrange for the youth group to visit children in a hospital or shelter.

34 Give a Kid a Smile

If there is a children's hospital in your area, visit the children and take them small gifts. The hospital can advise you on what gifts are acceptable or recommended. You may be able to take children's books and read to the kids. If you get their names and room numbers when you visit, you could send them a card or letter after you leave.

Youth: 3+

Time: 30–40 minutes

Supplies: Paper, scissors, a pen and pencil for each youth, three dictionaries (optional), three Bibles

Prep: Gather supplies. Cut out three small slips of paper and write the words *justice, kindness,* and *humility* on separate slips. If you have no dictionaries, type the definitions of the words on separate sheets of paper.

35 Micah 6:8 Acrostics

Read aloud Micah 6:8. If you have more than three youth, divide them into three groups. Give each person or group a dictionary or typed definition, a sheet of paper, a slip of paper, and a Bible.

Tell the youth to read the definition of the given word then write the word going down the left side of their sheets of paper. Allow them ten minutes to complete this task.

Say: "Now your group is going to create an acrostic of your assigned word. An acrostic is a series of phrases in which the first letter of each phrase forms a word, name, or message when read in sequence. For example, an acrostic for the word *hope* could read, 'helping other people everywhere.' You should write down only positive words, avoiding sarcasm and offensive language. The word written for each letter should somehow relate to Micah 6:8." Allow the youth a few minutes to create their acrostics.

When the youth are done, ask each group to show the acrostic to the full group and read aloud the dictionary's definition of the assigned word.

Finally, reread Micah 6:8 to the group. Take each of the following phrases and discuss with the group what they mean:

- to do justice

- to love kindness

- to walk humbly with your God

80

36 Prayerwalking

This powerful intercessory activity can be done in several ways. The people you choose to pray for can be from a designated list. You could also pray for a neighborhood, business, school, shelter, church, or any other group of people you want to focus on.

The idea is to walk the sidewalks and stop to pray at each home or building. No one else should know about this activity, so be discreet. The youth should offer prayer without any expectation of thanks or response.

You group may decide to do prayerwalking on a regular basis or on special occasions. After each session, spend a few minutes reflecting on your experience and how it feels to lift up others in prayer.

Youth: 3+

Time: 30 minutes to as many hours as you choose

Supplies: List of addresses of congregation members who are home-bound or families who need prayers; map (if needed)

Prep: Gather supplies and arrange transportation.

37 Affirmation Boxes

Create affirmation boxes and then place them in your youth group space where they can be used regularly. These containers will serve as personal mailboxes for the youth group. You may ask the youth to write or make something for others' boxes. Invite the youth to write notes to one another anytime they want and deposit them in the mailboxes. Let them know, however, that the notes and messages can only be positive. Affirmation boxes are not the place to discuss problems or issues between people. What the teens pull out of their mailboxes should build them up. Encourage them to write to every mailbox at least some of the time so that no one is left out.

Adult leaders can use these containers to send notes of congratulation or understanding, or to give small, inexpensive gifts (such as a candy bar, string of beads, Christmas ornament, pencil with the teen's name on it, and so forth).

Affirmation boxes also provide a good way to give the group printed material such as schedule reminders, forms to take home, a devotional magazine, weekly Scripture highlight, prayers, and so forth. Use your imagination!

Youth: 3+

Time: 45–60 minutes

Supplies: One container per person (shoe box, expanding file folder with side flap, or 1-gallon plastic milk jug); materials for decorating boxes (wrapping paper, crepe paper, markers, crayons, stickers, and so forth); tape and/or glue; markers for writing names (for milk jugs use permanent markers); plain paper; pen for each person

Prep: Gather supplies; wash out milk jugs if using them; cut out 4 small pieces of paper per person; have table(s) ready to work at

38 Follow the Leader

The purpose is to help youth learn to give clear, accurate, and descriptive instructions so that others can follow. Pick any game that fits the size of your group and have one youth read the instructions silently. Then he or she is to tell the others how to play.

If you don't have written instructions available to you, have the youth pick a game they already know, even one from childhood, choose a leader, and ask the group to do only what the leader says to do. If the youth skip a step or get confused, don't tell them how to get back on track. The group can either stop to discuss the mishap or start over with clarified instructions. If your group likes games, pick additional ones and have different youth give directions.

When the youth finish playing a game, ask the leaders to tell the others about how they felt while doing so, what frustrations they may have had, or how easy the task was. Ask the youth what would have happened if the leader had left out a certain step or described it incorrectly. When the group is finished discussing, have everyone clap for the leaders as a thank you for a job well done, no matter how they did the job.

39 Object Lesson

Using a prop to discuss symbolism makes teens more likely to tune in. Here is a sample object lesson:

Using the Power of God's Word

Pick a location where you can spray carbonated water without hurting anything. Have a bottle of carbonated water (not regular soda) ready with the top off.

Say, "This soda isn't very interesting or useful if we just let it sit here in the bottle." Put your thumb over the opening and shake up the bottle to make it fizz. Say: "But if I shake it up, the soda has a lot of power. Our faith is much the same way. If we just let it sit and do nothing with it, we aren't living up to our potential to do good in the world. But if we shake it up by studying, praying, and serving others, it can have enormous power."

Keep shaking the carbonated water then release your thumb to let it spray out. If you're outside on a warm day, you can surprise the youth by letting it spray over the group. When you spray the teens, say, "See how the power of God can reach others through us!"

40 On a Mission

Numerous service agencies are set up for youth groups to come to do mission work. They provide the housing, meals, and program. You just pay a registration fee for each person. Check with your denominational offices for some locations.

However, with a little more work and a lot less money, you can create your own trip and have experiences no one else will be having. My youth group enjoys going places no one else goes to. They know they can make a difference for the people they are serving. They realize that if we don't go there, the people will have no one. We often travel for a few days and stop in multiple locations to work. See page 20 for an example of a create-your-own mission trip.

Youth: 4+

Time: 3–5 days (depending on where you are going and travel time)

Supplies: Depends on project

Prep: Work with the youth to determine where they will be going and what kind of work they will be doing.

Here is a copy of a newsletter article from a church we visited on one of our trips:

> Our church was honored on Monday, 29 July, to have nine youth and three adults from the Portland area visit our church, do some "work around the house," and spend the night. They completely cleaned the basement, trimmed the bushes in front of the building, and did general grounds clean up. As a thank you, we hosted a potluck dinner; we shared stories and fellowship and they sang for us. Then they bedded down on the floor of the basement in their sleeping bags.
>
> The youth were on their way from the California Coast and thought this might be a good way to visit churches they'd never seen before, meet new people, do some good works, and earn their shelter for the night.
>
> Our thanks to everyone for providing the dinner and generally being hospitable to our visiting laborers. It was just like having our very own "youth group for a night"! What a joy it was to meet young people with a love of God, a desire to serve, and joy to share.
>
> We are so thankful for all the work they did for us, but most importantly, it did our hearts good.

This fellowship is a special reward for serving. It's also why we keep looking for small, out-of-the-way places to offer our hands and feet to the service of God's people, a service that also does our hearts good.

I encourage you to find a way to offer a mission trip experience for your youth group, no matter how small. On pages 84–85 is a Scripture-based youth group session for preparing to do mission work. Feel free to adopt it or to adapt it as you wish.

SERVANTS OF GOD:
MISSION TRIP SPIRITUAL DISCUSSION

CHANGE

Read aloud Matthew 9:35-38. Say: "Jesus says that God's kingdom is ready to expand. There's only one problem: There aren't enough laborers. This shortage leads to a lot of work for a few people.

"We will be serving others by helping bring about a positive change at the locations we choose to serve. What good might come of our service?"
(Physical: Doing labor for their physical buildings and grounds.
  Emotional: Creating a feeling of connectedness between churches and
      showing we care about others.
  Spiritual: We serve because we are called to serve.)

MODELS

Read aloud John 13:1-20. Say: "In this story Jesus washes the disciples' feet. This is not only a ritual of cleanliness similar to the washing of hands in our culture, but it is also a sign of Jesus' love for his disciples and symbolizes his role as a servant. Jesus instructs the disciples to do likewise and wash one another's feet. In other words, disciples of Jesus Christ are to serve one another." Ask:

• Who are your heroes?

• What do they model?

• What do as a Christian you model?

• What are some ways you might model the life of a servant?

• How will we show this attitude while working at our project sites?

• What will others around us see happening?

A SERVANT'S ATTITUDE

Read aloud Matthew 20:20-28. Say: "Two of Jesus' disciples, James and John, were the sons of Zebedee. Their mother asked a favor of Jesus. She wanted her sons to have a special place of honor in his kingdom. This request angered the other disciples. However, Jesus knew that they probably desired the same thing. So Jesus told them that if they wanted to be first, they had to be last. He said that they, like he, were to be servants.

"Sometimes we confuse our wants with our needs. God desires all people to have the things they truly need." Ask:

• What are some things you really need?
• How might some of these differ from the things you want?
• What does a servant of others desire?

MINISTRY

Read aloud James 1:22-25. Say: "The writer of James urges his preachers to not only hear the Word of God but to fulfill the Word as well. He says doers will be blessed in their doing."

Ask:

• What does it mean to you when you hear that all of God's people are called to be ministers?

Say, "Ministers are not just hearers; they are also doers." Ask:

  • What are some things you do well?
  • As a servant, are you willing to try to do new things to help others?

DOING AND BEING

Read aloud James 2:14-26. Say: "Faith must include works or it becomes lifeless. Faith includes what you think, feel, believe, and do. Being a faithful servant means using your head, your heart, and your hands." Ask, "What are some of your thoughts about being a servant?"

CLOSING PRAYER

"Use our minds, God, to think great thoughts of you and give you praise.

"Use our hearts, God, to feel compassion for others and a desire to serve in your name.

"Use our hands, God, to serve your people wherever we meet them.

"Our minds, our hearts, our hands we give to you, Lord. Bless them and use them to bless others. Amen."

41 In the Dark

Youth: 4+

Time: 30–40 minutes

Supplies: Table; 30–40 wooden blocks (children's blocks or scrap 2" x 4" chunks that are stackable and smoothed to minimize slivers); construction paper (any color); permanent marker for each person; masking tape; glow stick, candle and match, or mini flashlight for each person

Prep: Cut the construction paper into squares or rectangles that match the size of the blocks' sides. Place the paper cutouts, wooden blocks, marking pens, and tape in the middle of a table, with chairs on both sides facing each other. If your room cannot be darkened during the daytime, find a second space that can be darkened or do this activity at night.

Start by asking these questions:

- Do you know anyone who always seems unhappy?

- Have you ever lost a family member or friend?

- Do you ever feel as though you don't know how you'll get through something you know is ahead of you?

- Have you ever felt as though no one could possibly understand how angry, fearful, or lonely you feel?

Say: "People who are in difficult situations like these often feel cut off or blocked from the rest of the world, because their feelings have overwhelmed them. Some people choose to do destructive things to make the feelings go away. Others try to slowly but surely dig themselves out of the pit."

Divide the participants into two groups and have them sit across from each other at the table.

Say: "We have blocks that we are going to use to build a barricade or wall here on the table so that it divides or separates us from those across the table. I am going to ask you a question, and you will write your answers in words or short phrases on the paper and tape it to a block. Then place the block in the middle and stack the blocks into a wall as you go. The side on which you wrote should face away from you, so place each piece of paper you will write so that it faces the person across from you. Together we will build a 'wall of darkness.' "

Ask, "What are some words or phrases you would use to describe a person in darkness?" *(sad, evil, hating, angry, separated from God, far from light, without hope, alone, lonely, desperate, swallowed up, fearful, in pain, bereft, grieved, helpless, suffering, cut off from other people, withdrawn, depressed, overwhelmed, worthless, out of touch with reality).* Write your answer on a card and tape it to a block. Then place it on the wall we are building, using about half the blocks.

Now ask, "What are some situations, experiences, or feelings in your life, or the life of a friend or family member, that might bring on darkness? *(for example, loss, low self-esteem, death, fighting, shame, suffering, loneliness, broken relationships, poor choices, abuse, losing a job or friend, doing something wrong, being falsely accused, boredom, apathy, exhaustion)*

Allow the groups to write words on blocks until the blocks are all used and there is a small but definite wall between the two sides of the table.

Invite the group to discuss how real the wall feels and what it symbolizes for them. Ask:

- Do you have any walls or barriers keeping in the darkness that need to come down?

Go to the darkened space together. Have the group sit or stand in the dark, depending on how much space you have. Hand out the glow sticks (or alternative items), but ask that they just hold them for now and not light them. Once all of the group members have their glow sticks, ask them to be silent for one minute and think about how hard it would be to live in the dark for an extended length of time.

At the end of one minute, say: "How many things can you think of that can help someone overcome darkness? One person at a time, let's answer this question with a word or phrase. As you say your word or phrase, snap your glow stick to light it and hold it up for everyone to see. If you can't think of an idea, go ahead and use a word that's already been spoken." *(Some ways to overcome darkness may include light, faith, confidence, hope, God, Christ, friends, love, and kindness.)*

Continue until each person has lit his or her light. Ask:

- Do you have any new feelings or insights now that we have come from darkness to light?

- How can we be a light for one another and those around us?

- What gives us hope?

Pray this closing prayer: "God, Creator, we know that it is you who brings light into our darkness, hope into our despair, and love into our lives. Remind us that through you there is always a way out of the darkness. Help us to turn to you every day, for you are the light of our lives. Amen."

42 Prayer-a-Thon

Prayer-a-thon is my group's favorite activity of the year. Years ago I learned how to conduct it from other youth workers, and I keep adapting it every year. You can modify it any way you wish.

Begin by getting a commitment from the youth and adults to participate. You will need everyone possible. Give the youth permission slips, event descriptions, and schedules. Tell them they may each bring a pillow, slippers, or blanket, but not sleeping bags, because they will not be sleeping during the night.

After you reserve the prayer site, put prayer requests forms in the church bulletin, and prepare shoeboxes, it's time to make the schedule. Here's a sample one:

Prayer-a-Thon Schedule

Friday Evening

7:30	Participants arrive at church. Give instructions and hand out nametags with the schedules on the backs
7:50	Whole group goes to chancel area of sanctuary or chapel, lights candles, and has prayer together
8:00	Person/Group 1 begins reading prayer requests Everyone else is now in a nearby room with table games, books, homework, and so forth
8:15	Person/Group 2 Replaces 1 in sanctuary
8:30	Person/Group 3 Replaces 2 in sanctuary
8:45	Person/Group 4 Replaces 3 in sanctuary
9:00	Person/Group 5 Replaces 4 in sanctuary
9:15	Person/Group 1 Replaces 5 in sanctuary

Continue rotation all night until 7:45 A.M., with these exceptions:

12:00	Whole group does a 15-minute shift and reflects on it. Resume rotation.
2:00 and 2:30	The group goes outside for a walk to wake up (one-half of the group at a time so that the prayer isn't interrupted)

4:00	Whole group does a 15-minute shift and reflects on it. Then resume rotation.
7:45	Whole group does final 15 minutes together
8:00	Brief reflection time; ask:

- What was the best thing about this prayer-a-thon?

- What was the hardest?

- How do you feel about what we've done?

- What did you learn?

| 8:10 | Clean up, pack up |
| 8:30 | Goodbye |

The persons on the prayer shift read and pray any way they like. Everyone else has time for other activities together, but those praying should not be able to hear the others.

During the night, have everyone sign at least one prayer-a-gram sheet (see sample on page 90). After the event, make photocopies of the signed prayer-a-grams and send them out to everyone listed on request sheets with an address.

In the church newsletter or during the worship service's announcement time, thank the congregation for its participation.

Place announcements in the church newsletter, in the youth news, on bulletin boards, and any other place you can. Get a commitment from the youth to attend and their parent's permission in advance and remind the participants of what to bring. Gather the rest of the supplies.

Arrange for all night snacks and food options. Prepare the team assignments and rotation schedule for prayer. Make nametags with each individual's schedule on the back of it.

The night of the prayer-a-thon, collect the completed prayer request forms from the shoeboxes and put them in baskets or other containers. Put trays or some other protective covering on the floor in the center of the chancel area and put candles on the tray and the matches beside the candles. Put the prayer request sheets near the candles.

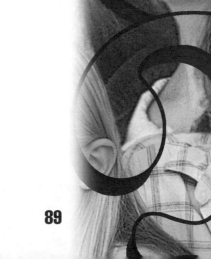

Prayer-a-Thon Request Form

✂

Dates of Prayer-a-Thon: _____ – _____

The youth of our congregation are holding a prayer-a-thon. Please support this event by writing a prayer request:

Please return this request form to the prayer box where you found it or mail it to _____.

During the prayer-a-thon, we will provide twelve hours of intercessory prayer dedicated to the requests. We also invite you to participate by praying with us from wherever you are during any of this time.

If you would like us to send a prayer-a-gram notifying someone of your prayer, please include his or her name and address here.

We would also like to hold you in prayer. If you are willing, please write your name and mailing address on the back of this form.

WHERE THERE IS PRAYER, THERE IS HOPE.

✂

Prayer-a-Gram

May God's love fill you, comfort you, and grant you peace.

"I AM WITH YOU ALWAYS, EVEN TO THE END OF THE AGE." —MATTHEW 28:20 (NLT)

We believe prayer has tremendous power. During our prayer-a-thon we have prayed for you, seeking God's response to your needs, concerns, and joys.

On (date) _____ we exchanged a night of sleep for the opportunity to come together and be in intercessory prayer for twelve hours. We may or may not know you personally, but please know that we care!

Sponsored by _____

_____ Church Youth

Youth leader and contact info:

_____

_____

Reproducible Descriptions and Forms

Registration (Page 98)

Even with a single-digit youth group, have the teens register to be part of the youth group. By requiring the youth to register, you'll know who has made a commitment to attend and who has not.

You'll also have more detailed information about the youths' home lives without having to interview them. Knowing whether the teens live with one parent, grandparents, an aunt and uncle, friends, or a sibling with a baby will help you understand their lives better and thus help you avoid inappropriate wording when you are with them. For instance, if you assume that each youth's household has a mom and a dad and you suggest making Father's Day gifts or cards, the youth without a father at home will feel awkward and left out. Although most youth think their living situation is normal, what is normal for individual teens may not be the norm for society or for you. So use the registration form to gather information on the teens' home life. That knowledge may or may not change how you approach the teen, but it might prevent you from making assumptions that negatively affect the youth group members.

Medical Authorization (Page 99)

A medical authorization form is one of the most important items to have for each participant in the youth group, including the adults. However, the forms will only be useful if you take all of them with you wherever the youth meet or travel. I recommend that you keep the originals in a travel packet that goes with you every time you take the youth off the church property. Also keep a set of copies in your regular meeting place. If you take more than one vehicle for activities, have a duplicate set of forms in each vehicle. They are only helpful if you have them available in a medically urgent situation.

In case of illnesses that are not medically urgent, always have with you a copy of the roster of participants. If you have their parents' names, addresses, and home and cell phone numbers available, you can call the parents to come and assist their child, should he or she become ill.

Check to see if your state has a time limit on medical authorization forms. Some states limit the forms' validity period to six months so that the information stays current. In this case, you may want to just send the parents new forms every six months. However, since doing so requires the parents to look up insurance and medical history information, some of them don't get the forms back to you on time. One way to make filling out forms easier is to prepare two forms, each with the appropriate dates six months apart to cover one year. Have the parents fill out both forms (but sign only the first one) and send them to you. Put them in two separate files, separated by the effective dates. A few weeks before the first one expires, send the second form to the parents so that they can review it, make and initial any changes or updates, sign it, and return it to you. This way, they

don't have to look up the insurance and medical history information twice.

Another way to cover the year is to make one form with two signature lines and date lines at the bottom. Have the parents sign only the first signature line and date it. A few weeks before the form expires, make a photocopy for your records and send the original to the parents for their review and update, asking them to sign the second signature line and date it. This procedure avoids having the parents fill out two separate forms yet gives them the opportunity to make sure the information is current and sign for the new time period. Page 99 provides a form you can use for one year or for two six-month periods.

Travel Information and Permission (Page 100)

I like to provide a form that gives the parents a full set of information related to the youth group travel plans. This set includes

- the title and destination of the trip,
- the dates and cost of the trip,
- where and when the youth are to meet and return,
- a list of what to bring,
- the name of the person in charge of the trip,
- how to reach the group in case of emergency (cell phone numbers),
- the schedule or agenda of the trip,
- what vehicles will be used,
- who will be driving, and
- the names of the adults traveling with the group.

This information shows them you are organized and have made the proper arrangements for the group with whom their children are traveling. Give the parents the travel information and permission form and ask that they cut apart, sign, and return the bottom half to you and keep the top so that they have the information. Page 100 provides a sample form based on the description above.

Volunteer Disclosure Form (Page 101)

This sample form from my youth ministry is similar to the one my conference uses in camp and retreat ministry. Every fall, I have the adults who will have any regular, direct contact with the teens in youth group complete the form, sign it, and turn it in to me. Anyone unwilling to do so will be unable to serve in contact with youth in our program. Anyone who answers yes to any of the questions will be asked to discuss this issue with the appropriate staff member. The staff will determine whether or not the item of discussion poses any potential danger to the youth the applicant will be working with.

For instance, if the applicant has a poor driving record, the staff may decide that he or she may work with the youth but may not be a driver for the youth group. The use of this form will not prevent the church or the youth leader from being sued. It does, however, show that the church has taken precautions by having disclosure and a safety policy to better assure safety for the children and youth. Another benefit of a disclosure form is that is may cause a person to self-select themselves out of volunteering, in which case they are doing you a favor.

I recommend you use some kind of disclosure form, whether it's the one on page 101, the volunteer application in *Safe Sanctuaries for Youth*, or your own version. Whichever you choose, have your church administration ask an attorney to review it to be sure it has wording that is appropriate in your setting. This sample will at least give you an idea of what kind of things to be checking.

Expectations of Participants (Page 102)

It is easy to get frustrated with youth who make poor choices or behave in a way that negatively affects the youth group. Sometimes youth seem to keep pushing the boundaries. But we often forget to be clear about what good choices and appropriate behaviors truly mean. We fail to tell the youth where the boundaries are until the teens go past them, upsetting us. Dealing with these behaviors after they have happened is much more difficult than making the rules clear ahead of time. There is no guarantee youth will avoid all of these behaviors, but they are less likely to do so if they  know the limits. Then if they still make poor choices, at least you have a tool or policy to work with in discussing the situation.

So I encourage you to give the youth a chance to succeed on their own by explaining the boundaries and asking them to honor those rules. They almost always will. On page 102 you will find a sample document you may

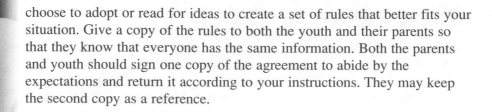

choose to adopt or read for ideas to create a set of rules that better fits your situation. Give a copy of the rules to both the youth and their parents so that they know that everyone has the same information. Both the parents and youth should sign one copy of the agreement to abide by the expectations and return it according to your instructions. They may keep the second copy as a reference.

Parental Permission (Page 103)

Getting written parental permission for an overnight, especially if it takes place at the church, may seem a bit excessive. But you should consider how well you know your youth and their parents when deciding whether to obtain this permission. I always want the parents know that their youth are

staying overnight away from home. It's even more important to make sure the parents are expecting their teens to be with the youth group. I learned this lesson the hard way: After I had asked a youth to tell her parents she was coming to the overnight, she told me she could come to only the first part and had to leave at a certain time. When she left, I thought she was returning home and the parents thought the youth was with me. This situation left the youth free to do whatever she wanted to do overnight.

I always hope that the youth are more honest than this girl was, but sometimes youth have difficulty resisting an opportunity to break rules. A parental permission form takes the guess work out of the situation. If you have received signed forms and a youth tells you he or she needs to leave, you can challenge the youth on the change of plans and call the parents to determine if they know what their child is planning to do. If you require permission slips for the youth who do attend and a youth who was supposed to be there gets hurt or arrested that night, the parents won't be telling you, "I thought my child was with you." The sample form of expectations of participants on page 102 addresses this liability issue.

For a parental permission form, see page 103. It is formatted for two copies per page, so you may print a page for each two youth and cut it in half.

Youth Group Roster

This sheet asks youth for information you may want to keep current. To make a youth group roster, you may want to use the following format:

Name: Grade:
Address: School:
City/State/Zip: Birth Date
Phone: Parent(s)
Cell: Work Phone:
E-mail: Notes:

You can adapt this format to whatever fits your needs, such as using a computer spreadsheet, which can be sorted by various fields. For safety and convenience, keep copies of the roster with the medical authorization forms in your meeting space and in the vehicles when your group is traveling. I use my group roster to develop additional lists by grade, birthday, and gender.

A roster also provides a good place to keep information on visiting youth or teens who have potential to attend youth group. You might even want to record dates you contact them.

Getting to Know You (Page 104)

I like to have the youth fill out a sheet of questions that helps me know some of their likes and dislikes. Having some random information about the youth can come in handy throughout the year. You may find ways to prepare surprises, use the information in a game, or start a discussion based on some answers. You can make up your own list of questions or use the reproducible list on page 104.

Study Topics Permission (Page 105)

You can use this form to get parents' permission for their children to participate in programs whose topics may be controversial. These issues may include topics of sexuality, teen pregnancy, adoption versus abortion, taking a public stand on a social issue, drugs and alcohol, sexually transmitted diseases, destructive cults, suicide, other religions, and so on. Because I feel that church is one of the safest places to explore life issues, there are no topics completely off limits to discussion in my youth group.

If a topic you haven't planned for comes up, you may need to ask the youth if you can schedule a session for that specific topic and explore it further. This method gives you the opportunity to inform the parents on what topics will be explored, and it lets the parents express concern or give permission for their teens to participate.

In some cases, you may decide to invite the parents to attend part or all of a session or a series of sessions. For instance, if you are studying abortion in several sessions, you may welcome the parents to hear guest speakers for the first few sessions, which will inform them on what their children hear. This openness usually takes the fear out of the topic. On the other hand, you may decide the parents will not be invited when the youth group gets into the follow-up, heavy, and more personal discussions.

If you have a very small youth group, you may want to take the youth to the speakers rather than bring in speakers. For instance, if the first step in studying

> ### It Worked for Us: Obtaining Study Permission
>
> Years ago, a parent gave me permission for a youth to participate in a study on abortion only if I would tell the group what stance to take and what they should believe—and that it should be what those particular parents believed. I refused to approach the discussion this way, since I wanted the youth to have all the information they could get and then form their own opinions on what was right or wrong.
>
> The parents chose to attend the sessions and participated actively in the debate. Their opinions were heard, yet the group was also able to have an appropriate discussion.

abortion is to be sure the youth understand what an abortion physically involves, you can't assume that every youth, or even adult, knows what all the procedure involves. So perhaps you can visit a doctor in his or her clinic on an evening or Sunday afternoon for this conversation. Get creative about how to obtain the information from professionals so that the group can have an informed conversation. With a topic like abortion, the youth need to form their ideas and opinions based on information and their faith rather than pressure and fear. It is possible that sooner or later they or someone they know will need to deal with decisions of abortion, adoption, or raising a child. Discussing the topic in youth group gives them a head start in preparing themselves for life's potential challenges.

Of course, not every study topic is as controversial as abortion, so you will need to determine the degree of preparation and notification or permission needed from topic to topic. Remember that these kinds of studies may cause ripples or even explosions among parents if they are not informed and included in the decision of whether their children will participate. So just be up front and open about what the group is going to do, avoiding surprises that could be controversial.

Event or Activity Planning Worksheet (Page 106)

Anytime the youth group decides to have an event or activity beyond its usual meeting format, you may want to use a planning worksheet. This sheet will help you keep track of which tasks are done, what is left to work on, and who is taking responsibility for various items. You'll feel less pressure when you don't have to wonder whether you've forgotten something. If additional information is determined or specific program information is planned, you may simply use the back of this form to include that information so that it's all in one place. I encourage you to use this sheet or something similar that suits your style of planning.

Prayers Worksheet (Page 107)

I Thessalonians 5:17 reminds us to always pray, without ceasing, in all that we do. As Christians we know that we need God in our lives, so prayer is always a good idea. One way you can support your youth group is to pray for them every day. This sheet may help you remember which people and concerns need prayers. It will also help you keep your youth and their families in prayers throughout the year in addition to the times when issues arise. These recommended categories can be changed to meet your needs.

Interest Survey of Youth Group Program Topics (Pages 108–109)

I used to begin each school year by asking the youth what they wanted to learn or experience that year. I often got blank stares, a lot of hesitation, or "I don't know" answers. Some people have difficulty thinking of ideas right on the spot without some kind of prompting. So I started developing a long list of topics for youth to consider.

I give them each a printed list and ask them to circle their five favorites from each of the four categories. I also invite them to cross out topics they are tired of or have no interest in. The rest should just be left alone. I gather all of the sheets and tally up the results. This gives me a pretty good idea of what topics to include that year as well as a second set of topics to include if we have space to fill during a program, retreat, or mission trip. In ten to fifteen minutes the youth can mark their sheets and be finished. I also ask the youth to fill out my activities survey the same way. In one meeting time we can develop our two lists and begin to plug those into our calendar for the year. This process is much less frustrating and can also spark new ideas.

Interest Survey of Youth Group Activities (Pages 110–111)

As with the program topics, this list helps the youths identify their preference of activities for the year. I invite them to circle each of their top five choices then put an X by each of their second five choices. In scheduling activities, I try to alternate between ones that involve learning or serving others and ones that are entertainment or recreation oriented. I also alternate between activities that cost money and those that do not. Some youth may not be able to afford the former kind of activities very often, so be aware of your teens' financial situation. As time allows, use the activities the teens have marked as priorities. These activities are important for building relationships and deepening relationships within the group. The closer they feel to one another, the more willing they will be to risk being open in their conversations with fellow group members.

Registration: _____ Youth Group

Participant Name _____ School Year _____ – _____

Address _____ City/State _____ Zip _____

Phone ( ) _____ Cell ( ) _____ E-mail _____

Birth Date _____ Grade _____

Have you been baptized? _____ Yes _____ No

If baptized elsewhere, write name and city of church: _____

Have you joined in "membership" at a church? _____ Yes _____ No

If yes, write name and city of church: _____

In what church groups or committees do you participate?

In what school or community groups do you participate?

Are there specific days and times of the week you are NOT available to do youth group activities? (Please list here.)

Do you have food restrictions (including vegetarian)? (Please list and explain if the restriction is serious.)

Adults in Your Home

Name_____ Relationship _____

Work _____ Work Phone _____

Other phone (cell/pager) _____ E-mail _____

Name_____ Relationship _____

Work _____ Work Phone _____

Other phone (cell/pager) _____ E-mail _____

Complete and send form to: _____

Medical Authorization Form

Event/Group Name _____

Sponsored by (church and city) _____

Participant's name: _____ Date of Birth _____/_____/_____ Sex _____

Street Address _____ Youth: Age _____ Grade _____

City _____ State _____ Zip _____ Adult: _____

Home Phone ( ) _____ Cell Phone ( ) _____

Allergies / special health concerns / medications / dietary needs:

_____

Date of last tetanus shot: _____/_____/_____

Surgery or Serious Illness History _____

Physician's Name _____ Physician's Phone ( ) _____

Insurance Company _____ Insured's Name _____

Policy Number _____ ID Number: _____

Parents: My child may participate in the above stated event/group, including travel during the event via church vehicle or automobile driven by an adult chaperone/leader who is age 21 or older with a valid driver's license. I give permission for my child/myself to receive emergency medical care if necessary. I give the adult chaperones/leaders the authority to act on my behalf with respect to my child's/my own health and safety while at the event, with the understanding that I/emergency contact listed above will be contacted as soon as possible should the need arise. I accept full responsibility for any expenses for medical treatment for my child/myself. I release _____ Church and its representatives from liability in the event of accidental injury or illness.

Effective Dates: From _____ to _____. Date _____ (6 months) Signed _____ (Parent/guardian or adult participant age 21 or over) Print _____	Effective Dates: From _____ to _____. Date _____ (6 months) Signed _____ (Parent/guardian or adult participant age 21 or over) Print _____

Emergency phone numbers: ( ) _____–_____   ( ) _____–_____

Travel Information and Permission

Group name and church: _____

Dates of travel: _____

Name and/or type of event: _____

Leaving from_____ at _____ on _____.
               (location)   (time)   (day and date)

Itinerary (Plan for each day, including when, where, what):

Returning to _____ at _____ on _____.

Cost: _____   Partial Scholarships are____ / are not____ available for this event.

Questions? Contact _____ at _____ or _____
                                (phone)   (2nd phone or e-mail)

What to bring:

How to reach the group in case of an emergency: _____

-- ✂

Registration for _____
                      (Event Name)

To register, fill out this permission slip and give/send with a $_____check payable to

_____ as soon as possible and no later than_____
                                       (day and date)

to _____.
               (name and address)

For parent or adult participant to complete and return:

Please reserve a space for _____ to attend this event/activity.
                        (name)

I understand that the medical authorization form previously submitted for this participant will be in effect and used if an emergency arises during this event.

For youth participant: Parent/Guardian _____ _____ Date: _____
                                   (sign)   (print)

For adult participant: _____ _____ Date: _____
                    (sign)   (print)

Volunteer and Staff Disclosure Form

Church name and city _____

Name of volunteer _____

Phone number(s) (____) _____   (____) _____

Street address _____

City/state _____ Zip _____

MISSION STATEMENT

The purpose of youth ministry is to provide communities of belonging through which youth can explore and affirm who they are as gifted people of God and actively live out their Christian faith within the body of Christ and all of God's creation.

I agree to serve toward the fulfillment of this mission as an adult worker with youth while participating in _____ _____ Church's sponsored youth events or groups.

As an expression of this mission, the church desires to ensure the well-being of all who participate, especially children, youth, vulnerable adults, and developmentally challenged persons. Joining with parents, legislative bodies, and youth organizations, we support requiring disclosures by all adults. Adults who desire to be involved in a church youth event or group must fill out this form completely and return it to

_____.

HISTORY

(Please answer yes or no. Attach an explanation for each yes.)

a. Have you ever been convicted for the possession, use, or sale of drugs? _____

b. Have you ever been convicted of a crime against children or other persons? _____

c. Have you ever been convicted of a felony? _____

d. Is there any fact or circumstance involving you or your background that would call into question your being entrusted with the supervision, guidance, and care of children, youth, or adults? _____

e. Has your driver's license been suspended or revoked within the past three years? _____

f. Within the past thirty days, have you drunk too much alcohol or abused legal or illegal drugs? _____

g. Have you ever been reviewed by church (including youth and camp/retreat ministries) and/or secular bodies and been restricted from involvement with children, youth, or adults? _____

I understand that as a person in authority within the ministry of _____ Church, it is my responsibility to avoid sexual or other inappropriate contact with children, youth, and adults during and going to or from events or group gatherings with youth. I will uphold this responsibility even if someone other than me attempts to initiate the contact. Under no circumstance will I use corporal punishment as a means of discipline.

I certify that the information I have provided is true and correct. I understand that _____ Church reserves the right to exclude my participation if it has found that the answers given above are inaccurate or if I am accused of abusive or dangerously irresponsible behavior.

Exclusion from participation in youth events or groups will continue until an official review is completed. The purpose of a review is to examine the situation and determine whether future participation in church-sponsored youth events or groups will be permitted and under what conditions.

Signature _____

Date _____

Expectations of Participants

Because we are a caring Christian community, we ask that youth and their parents read and sign the following expectations:

🐚 No youth will leave any group activity early, especially an overnight activity, without a parent picking him or her up and contacting the youth director in advance. If a youth leaves, we cannot be responsible for him or her while he or she is absent. Youth may not come and go during activities. If they leave, they may not return unless prior arrangements have been made with the youth director.

🐚 We insist that participants refrain from use of tobacco, alcohol, narcotic drugs, offensive language, and personal listening devices during meetings and activities. Exceptions for personal listening devices during overnights, retreats, or trips will be determined by leaders and explained as necessary.

🐚 Equipment (video and audio) are for program purposes and are to remain off unless specific permission is given.

🐚 We ask that participants help keep our meeting spaces clean and neat. We should always leave our rooms at least as clean as we found them. All participants will be asked to assist with this task.

🐚 Photographs are taken during many of our gathering times. (Some photos may be submitted for publication elsewhere, such as the church's newspaper.) If there is some safety reason any youth should not have his or her photo available for others to see, please indicate this reason on the next page so that we can talk about limits.

🐚 Individual contact information, including e-mail addresses, are also provided for the youth group participants and their church. If there is any safety reason this distribution is not acceptable, please indicate this reason on the next page and feel free to contact the youth leader to discuss any concerns.

🐚 Participants are asked to follow this agreement and the youth group covenant any time we are together as a partial or full group. Christian hospitality, respect, and courtesy are expected of group members to help make our time together as safe and meaningful as possible.

🐚 Youth are welcome to bring a friend to regular meeting times. Special events may require the friend to attend our regular meetings at least two times within the four weeks prior to the special event. The adults supervising our youth need the opportunity to recognize and, if possible, know the youth they are being asked to supervise. Exceptions may be made for new group members but not for visitors.

🐚 Mission trip participants are expected to help with at least seventy-five percent of the fundraising activities or to pay additional fees in order to attend the event. Negotiations may be made with the youth director.

🐚 Confidentiality and trust are important to our developing a safe environment when difficult issues may be discussed. We ask that personal information not be shared outside the group unless issues of safety are involved.

🐚 Persons under twenty-one years of age may not drive during youth group activities. All drivers must be twenty-one or over and hold a current driver's license.

I have read and agree to the expectations stated above.

Participant's signature _____

and printed name _____

Date: _____

Parent/Guardian signature _____

and printed name _____

Date: _____

Please sign and return to:

_____

Parental Permission

My child, _____, has my permission to attend the youth group activity on (dates) _____, and I give the adults leaders of the youth group authority to act on my behalf if my child should need emergency medical care. The information on my child's medical authorization form is complete and accurate and may be used should the need arise. I understand that I will be contacted as soon as possible if health or safety issues warrant action to be taken. I can be reached at the numbers below during the above dates.

I understand the group expectations of participants will be enforced, especially this policy:

Youth may not leave any group activity early, especially overnights, without their parent picking them up and contacting me in advance. If a youth leaves, we cannot be responsible for him or her while he or she is absent. Youth may not come and go during activities. If they leave, they may not return, unless prior arrangements have been made with the director. (Parents will be called if a youth leaves and no prior arrangements have been made.)

Signed _____ Date _____
                     (parent or guardian)

Emergency contact phone numbers: _____

_____ ✂

Parental Permission

My child, _____, has my permission to attend the youth group activity on (dates) _____, and I give the adults leaders of the youth group authority to act on my behalf if my child should need emergency medical care. The information on my child's medical authorization form is complete and accurate and may be used should the need arise. I understand that I will be contacted as soon as possible if health or safety issues warrant action to be taken. I can be reached at the numbers below during the above dates.

I understand the group expectations of participants will be enforced, especially this policy:

Youth may not leave any group activity early, especially overnights, without their parent picking them up and contacting me in advance. If a youth leaves, we cannot be responsible for him or her while he or she is absent. Youth may not come and go during activities. If they leave, they may not return, unless prior arrangements have been made with the Director. (Parents will be called if a youth leaves and no prior arrangements have been made.)

Signed _____ Date _____
                     (parent or guardian)

Emergency contact phone numbers: _____

_____

Getting to Know You

Name _____

Do you have a nickname? _____ If yes, what is it? _____

Your favorite quiet activity in your leisure time is_____.

If everything in your life were only one color, what color would it be? _____

What band or music group do you most enjoy? _____

What one book would you recommend that your friends read? _____

Describe the best thing about your bedroom. _____

What pets do you have and what are their names? _____

What's your favorite outdoor activity? _____

Which pizza toppings do you like best? _____

Who is the teacher you learned the most from? _____

How many siblings do you have? _____

Where have you traveled to? _____

What's your favorite amusement park ride? _____

What is your favorite flavor of ice cream? _____

Do you prefer the mountains or the ocean? _____

What's your favorite Christmas tradition? _____

What one question would you most like answered by God? _____

Would you prefer to play your favorite sport or watch it? _____

If you could change one thing about yourself, what would it be? _____

What's your favorite food? _____

What's something you're really good at? _____

What else would you like to say about yourself? _____

Study Topic Permission

The youth group of _____ Church
has selected the topic of _____
 for in-depth study and discussion.

The youth will be gathering information and hearing various points of view in an effort to be fully informed. Then they will launch into discussion about the facts of the topic, their thoughts about it, and how their faith influences their responses.

It is important for youth to explore many different life issues in light of their faith, and we want the parents to know what we are studying. Since there is potential controversy with this subject matter, we ask your permission for your teen to participate in this youth group study. If you have concerns, please contact _____ at _____ for conversation or further information.

Permission:

My child, _____, has my permission to participate in the above study topic with the youth group. I understand that group conversations, especially on sensitive subjects, are held confidential within the group unless a safety issue that needs to be handled beyond the group arises.

Signed _____

Print Name _____

Date _____

Event or Activity Planning Worksheet

Date:

Location:

　Address/room number:

　Phone number:

Facility or room reservations needed?

Facility cost?

Type or title of the event:

Objective (the purpose and desired result):

Beginning time:

Ending time:

Persons in charge:

　Adult:

　Youth:

Helpers: (Who and what?)

Who's invited?

Number of people expected: _____

Permission form needed?

　Yes____　If so, is it prepared?____

　No____

What and who are our resources?

Materials/supplies needed? _____

　If so, what are they and who is bringing them?

Cost to group and/or church: _____

Cost/fee for participants: _____

Prayers Worksheet

"Pray without ceasing."
–1 Thessalonians 5:17

As Christians we know we need God in our lives, so there is never a time when prayer isn't a good idea! Here is a place to keep a list of specific prayers as well as general prayers:

List names and needs to pray about.

Youth Group:

Individual Youth:

Youth Group Families:

Church Community:

Neighbors:

Government Leaders:

Friends:

Personal:

Interest Survey of Youth Group Program Topics[1]

The Bible and Faith

All About Jesus

Back-to-the-Bible Basics

Being a Faithful Disciple

The Christmas Story

Creation and Creating

Do Miracles Really Happen?

Elements of Worship

Freedom: What Is It, and Where Do I Get It?

Fruit of the Spirit

Getting Closer to God

God's Forgiveness

The Grace of God: What Is It?

Hope for the Future

I Have Doubts and Questions

Lent: What and Why?

The Lord's Prayer—Paraphrased

The Music of Life

Other Religions

The Parables

Prayer and Meditation

Resurrection

Sacraments: What Do They Mean?

Symbols of Our Faith

Temptation

Unsolved Mysteries of the Bible

What Does Holy Communion Mean?

What Is Faith?

What Is Pentecost?

Where Do We See God?

Who Is God?

Who Is the Holy Spirit?

Individual Issues and Faith

Accepting Myself and Others

Being in Leadership

Being Shy Can Be Tough

Dealing With Stress

Decision-Making—What to Do?

Eating Disorders—Who Can Help?

Feeling Angry: Finding Positive Solutions

Getting Organized

How Can I Overcome Fear?

I'm So Bored!

In Search of Meaning in My Life

I Worry About . . .

Leaving Home After Graduation

Learning to Really Listen

Living for Better Health and Fun

Making My Own Space

Materialism—I Want . . .

My Bedroom

My Unique Gifts From God

Survey of Youth Program Topics, Continued

Preparing for Adulthood

Setting Goals and Dreams

Sticky Situations: Do I Cop Out or Do I Cope?

Suicide: Feelings, Signs, Resources

Taking Responsibility for My Actions

Taking Risks

What if I Fail?

What? Me a Minister?

What's My Self-Image?

When I Feel Like Giving Up

When I'm Lonely

Why Do I Do What I Do? Values and Behaviors

Relationships and Faith

Conflict Resolution

Dating: What's It All About?

Deepening Relationships

Facing My Mistakes

Forgiveness, Comfort, Encouragement

Gift Giving

Gossip: Taming the Tongue

In All Honesty . . .

Loving Those We Don't Even Like

My Family's a Mess

People I Admire and Why

Saying Thank You

Sensuality, Sexuality, and Faith

Stereotypes and Labeling

Those Weird Things Parents Do

The Walls I Build

What Does God Want Me to Do?

What if Mom or Dad Dies?

What Is This Thing Called Love?

You Are Not Alone

Social Issues and Faith

Advertising Messages

AIDS—Important Questions

Bumper-Sticker Hunt

Christians and Drinking

Diversity: Appreciating Our Differences

Following the Rules

Healthy Competition

Homelessness

Hunger: Can I Make a Difference?

Other Cultures: Lifestyles, Music, and More

Poverty and Missions

Taking Care of God's Creation

Teen Parenting

My Denomination's Social Principles

War

What's News? The Media

When Should I Speak Out?

[1]Reprinted from *Twists of Faith: Ministry With Youth at the Turning Points of Their Lives* by Marcey Balcomb and Kevin Witt. Copyright © 1999 Discipleship Resources. All rights reserved. Used by permission.

Interest Survey
of Youth Group Activities

Adopt-a-Grandparent (Hear their stories)

Attend one another's school plays, concerts, games, and so on

Awards and Celebrations (Everyone Wins!)

Bake-Over (sell bread or give to a shelter or to people who are homebound)

Banana Split Night (everyone bring toppings)

Barbecue

Beach Day (sandcastles, kites, and so forth)

Bible Pictionary®

Boating/Canoeing

Bowling

Camp-Out (tents)

Candle Making and/or Decorating

Christian Concerts

Christmas Lights Tour

Christmas Wrapping Party or Service

Clay Play

Collect Litter in City/County Park

Computer Games Party

Conference Sponsored Events

Create a Recycling Center or Program

Create Storybook for Children in the Congregation

Create Youth Group Photo Album or Scrapbook

Destination Unknown

District Sponsored Events

Dog Wash

Easter Egg Dying or Egg Hunt for Children

Faith Retreat

Favorite Books Night

Games Night (table games, water games, and so forth)

Go Out for a Nice Dinner

Habitat for Humanity (help build a house)

Help With Vacation Bible School

House/Yard Work for Older Adults or People With Disabilities

Ice Cream Party

Ice Skating

Journaling Retreat

Lead Children's Time/Story in Worship

Lead Worship

Local Service Project

Lock-In at Church

Make and Send Valentines (or other seasonal cards) to People Who Are Homebound

Mission Trip

Mother's Day Bouquets

Movie Madness or Marathon

Museums

Mystery Night

Neighborhood Clean-Up

Painting Party (clean up graffiti)

Parachute Games (6–9 people)

Parents' Day Out (care for children at church)

Pen Pals With Youth in Russia or Africa

Picnic

Pizza Sale (make unbaked to order)

Plant Bedding Plants in the Spring for Church Members

Prayer-a-Thon

Programs for Retirement Center or Nursing Home

Rafting

Regressive Dinner (start with dessert)

Retreat Weekend

Roller Skating

Scavenger Hunt

Serve Cookies at Coffee Hour

Serve in Homeless Shelter

Serve on Homeless Food/Soup Line

Singing Favorite Songs (from radio or camp songs)

Skiing and Tubing

Snow-Shoveling Services

Souper Bowl of Caring (collection and service blitz)

Sponsor a Children's Craft Time (after church)

Study Hall (together before finals)

Sub Sandwich Party

Super Bowl Sandwiches (take orders and deliver)

Swimming

Theme Foods Night (Mexican, finger foods, potatoes)

Urban Campout (near the church or in someone's backyard)

Usher and/or Greet at Church

Valentine's Day Dinner for Youth Group

Visit Nursing Home and Decorate for the Residents

Visit Children in a Local Hospital (skits, reading storybooks, and so forth)

Visiting Other Churches/Non-Christian Houses of Worship

Work Party at a Church Camp

Write Thank-You Notes/Letters

Zoo

Wrap-Up

Youth need and deserve the support of adult advocates, mentors, listeners, teachers, and pastors in the church. Each teenager should have the opportunity to belong to a community and, if possible, to share that experience with their peers. Our former way of thinking dictated that a youth group needed a critical mass of people before it could be viable and function successfully. Now we challenge that premise so that we can minister to youth in whatever ways that can create meaningful, safe, and healthy relationships. More importantly, we use whatever ways we can to introduce them to the One who loves them more than we can imagine.

Our youth need opportunities to explore and affirm who they are as gifted people of God. We have the honor of guiding them as they learn to actively live out their faith. We can be the hands and feet of God in this place and time, and we can work alongside our youth in serving others and relaying our stories.

As teenagers, they aren't far from venturing out on their own, and the foundation of their faith will sustain them and carry them into new and exciting stages of their lives. Let's be there for them so that they're ready for what lies ahead.

Resources

Destination Unknown: 50 Quick Mystery Trips for Youth Groups. Halverson, Sam. Abingdon Press, 2001; ISBN: 0-687-09724-X.

Devo'Z. Nashville: Upper Room Ministries. ____ an order, call 1-800-7____

DATE DUE

Faith-F____ ____. Dyson, Drew A. Abingd____

ileadyo____ ____ youth ministry, as well as ____, and other lessons to use a____ ____ on youth resources.

Safe Sa____ ____ *in Youth Ministri____* ____s, 2003; ISBN: 0-88177____

Sage Ad____ ____lenwaters, Scott. Abingd____

10 Thin____ ____*istry.* Pletcher, Reuelly____

Tween T____ ____s. Abingdon Press, 2003; I____

Tween T____ ____ens. Abingdon Press, 2____

Twists o____ ____s of Their Lives. Balcom____ ____es, 1999; ISBN: 0-88177____

PRINTED IN U.S.A.

Fewer Than Ten Teens